poetry in crosslight

By the same author:

Poetry

Modern Poets XI (Penguin)
Two Voices (Cape Goliard)
Logan Stone (Cape Goliard)
Love and Other Deaths (Paul Elek)

Anthology

The Granite Kingdom (Barton)

poetry in crosslight

D M THOMAS

Longman

LONGMAN GROUP LIMITED

London and New York

Associated companies, branches and representatives
throughout the world

Longman Group Limited
This Collection © Longman Group Limited 1975

First published 1975

ISBN 0 582 48351 4 cased
      0 582 48352 2 paper

Library of Congress Catalog Card Number: 73-93353

Set in 11 on 12 pt. Monotype Baskerville
and printed in Great Britain by
Western Printing Services Ltd, Bristol

Contents

Part II: QUARRY AND FIGURE: *poems and variations*

Acknowledgements

We are grateful to the following for permission to reproduce copyright material:
Anthropos Editions St-Paul for an extract from 'Evening Quietness' in *The Flowers of the Year* (1912) by F. Dunn of Anthropos VII; Author's Agents for an extract from 'The Ballad of Charlotte Dymond' in Johnny Alleluia by Charles Causley. Published by Rupert Hart Davies; A. S. Barnes & Company Inc. for the poem 'A Mother to her First Born' from *Initiation: Translations From Poems of the Didinga and Lango Tribes* by Jack Herbert; Jonathan Cape Ltd. for an extract from '85' in *Catullus* translated by Louis and Celia Zukofsky. Published by Cape Goliard Press; Jonathan Cape Ltd. and Holt, Rinehart and Winston Inc. for the poem 'Come In' and extracts from 'How Hard It Is To Keep From Being King When It's In You' and 'In The Situation' from *The Poetry of Robert Frost* edited by Edward Connery Lathem. Copyright 1942 © 1962 by Robert Frost. Copyright © 1969 by Holt, Rinehart and Winston Inc. Copyright © 1970 by Lesley Frost Ballantine. Reprinted by permission of Holt, Rinehart and Winston Inc. and the Estate of Robert Frost; Jonathan Cape Ltd. and Farrar, Strauss & Giroux Inc. for an extract from *The Heights of Macchu Picchu* by Pablo Neruda. Reprinted by permission of Farrar, Strauss & Giroux and the Estate of Pablo Neruda. Copyright © 1966 by Jonathan Cape Ltd. Translation © 1966 by Nathaniel Tarn; Faber and Faber Ltd. and Farrar, Strauss & Giroux Inc. for an extract from 'Orpheus Eurydice and Hermes' in *Imitations* by Robert Lowell. Reprinted by permission of Farrar, Strauss & Giroux Inc. and Faber and Faber Ltd. Copyright © 1958, 1959, 1960, 1961 by Robert Lowell; The Clarendon Press for extracts from *Between the Lines* by Jon Stallworthy 1963. Copyright © 1963 Oxford University Press. Reprinted by permission of The Clarendon Press, Oxford; Faber and Faber Ltd. and Harcourt Brace Jovanovich Inc. for the poem 'Marina' from *Collected Poems* 1909–1962 by T. S. Eliot. Copyright 1963 by Harcourt Brace Jovanovich Inc. © 1963, 1964 by T. S. Eliot. Reprinted by permission of the publishers; Faber and Faber Ltd. and Harper & Row Publishers Inc. for 'The Thought-Fox' from *Hawk In The Rain* by Ted Hughes Copyright © 1957 by Ted Hughes. Originally appeared in *The New Yorker*. Reprinted by permission of Harper & Row Publishers Inc.; Faber and Faber Ltd. and Random House Inc. for 'The Idea of Order at Key West' in *Collected Poems* by Wallace Stevens. Copyright 1936 by Wallace Stevens and renewed 1964 by Holly Stevens. Reprinted by permission of Alfred A. Knopf Inc.; William Collins Son & Co. Ltd. and Random House Inc. for the two poems 'Winter Night' and 'The Wind' from *Doctor Zhivago* by Boris Pasternak, translated by Max Hayward and Manya Harari. Copyright © 1958 by William Collins Son & Co.

Introduction

A poem is able to catch at our breaths by leaping across huge gulfs of experience and making nothing of them. The poet's special freedom, says Robert Frost, is 'the freedom to fly off into wild connections'. The first poem in this book leaps across the distance separating a rat and a star, and binds them into a palindrome, 'rat's star'. The last poem in the book shows us, not a man singing, but a song walking. At the dawn of western civilization, Aristotle was already stating that metaphor was the most important element in poetry.

The 'wild connection' extends beyond the agreed limits of metaphor. It also exists in the harmonious tension between content and form, between the chaos of experience and the order of art. An elaborate verse pattern used for pastoral themes in seventeenth-century France; an old man dying in Wales in the middle of the twentieth century: how can they connect? But they do, in Dylan Thomas's villanelle, *Do not go gentle into that good night*.

A poem resembles a double or multiple star, sustained by a balance of centrifugal and centripetal forces. A close analysis can reveal the separate elements in isolation; but as soon as we take our eyes from the telescope all we can see is one clear particular star. A poem, in fact, is a small image of the universe, its multiplicity and its unity.

This book is an attempt to allow its readers to share something of this experience, by 'bonding' poems and other related texts. In seeing a poem under crosslights from other connected but unique texts, readers will, I hope, begin to breathe some of the poet's metaphoric excitement.

There are five parts, corresponding to different kinds of connection:

I. DISTILLATIONS. Poems are set beside prose passages associated with them in some way: diary entries; letters; excerpts from poets' novels; poets' informal discussions.

II. QUARRY AND FIGURE. Poems and early drafts; examples of the way poems are carved out of the raw material. Poems in variant forms, left undecided by the poets themselves or by the confusions and corruptions of time.

III. CROSSINGS. Translations, either of the letter or the spirit. Other crossings, where completely original poems stand in a specially close relationship to each other.

IV. WHITE SONG, BLACK INK. Poems related in theme or mood, from oral cultures – primitive societies or our own traditional poetry – and from 'advanced' recorded cultures.

V. GHOST IMAGES. Poems which, whatever else they express, are in part about themselves. The related texts are here focused into one, though with a 'ghost image' such as we sometimes find on a television screen or record. There is a poem about a work of art – say, a Grecian urn; and there is a poem that is itself a work of art—*Ode on a Grecian Urn*.

Notes are attached to all the groupings, giving, where appropriate, background information and critical ideas. The latter are kept to a minimum: just enough to open a way into a difficult poem or to provide a starting point for a classroom or seminar discussion, without any sense of certainties. It is for the readers to make their own explorations. Poetry wears many masks; I hope that now and again its living face will be caught and illuminated, like an actor, in these crosslights.

D. M. THOMAS

Part I

distillations

prose and poetry

1[a] DISCUSSION BETWEEN GEORGE MACBETH AND ANNE SEXTON ON HER POEM *With Mercy for the Greedy*

M: One of the things that's particularly interesting about this is the dedication, I think, and the poem's preoccupation with religion. Were you brought up in any particular religion very strictly?

S: Yes, a Protestant one.

M: In your poems there sometimes seems to be a special sort of preoccupation with ritual; of a sort that I suppose is not very common in Protestantism.

S: No, I think I'm rather attracted to Catholicism. And everyone thinks I was a Catholic and left the Church and now I tell everyone that I'm an atheist. No one knows what I am, but I think I have a great preoccupation with Catholicism. All on my own with no influence whatever.

M: It's interesting you can say, well, I'm an atheist quite surely and at the same time have this preoccupation —

S: This is an obsession, though, you see. And I'm not sure where it leads to. And I even answer it in this poem by saying, it is poems that have done it for me, poems are my religion. That's my answer in the poem.

M: You do come back, not only in this poem but in some others, though, to very realistic details about certain features of Christianity like the crucifixion. You say 'There is a beautiful Jesus, he is frozen to his bones like a chunk of beef'; well, this reminds one of certain sorts of very moving religious paintings, in which the actual physical suffering of Christ on the cross is very present.

S: Well, I am very aware of this. All the time I am very influenced by Christ, and the physical suffering. Perhaps more attracted to the suffering than the rising.

M: It's the human side of it, in fact, the person —?

S: Yes, the human being there on the cross.

M: But you have never felt moved to become converted to Catholicism or to any other religion?

S: I have thought of it and even tried it, but it hasn't worked. I'm still a sceptic.

M: Indeed, this poem is about —

S: About that. Being a sceptic. But saying, all I have to give
      to Christ is my poem. Really that's what I say.

M: Of course, the last lines of the poem are, in a curious way,
      very gnomic and hard to interpret. 'This is what poems
      are: / with mercy / for the greedy, / they are the tongue's
      wrangle, / the world's pottage, the rat's star.' In a curious
      way they resound in the mind without one's being abso-
      lutely clear what you have in mind, particularly this
      phrase 'the rat's star', which is a palindrome, isn't it?

S: Yes, it is a palindrome, yes.

M: Star is rat's backward —

S: But a rat is the most evil thing, and if you found his star,
      then you might find a few poems on it.

M: M'mm. So it's something about —

S: It would be all right, then, to be on the rat's star. That's
      about where the poems end up.

M: It's something about finding stars everywhere —

S: Well, against religion, I mean saying that Christ rose, and
      he was indeed beautiful and saved us all, poems just go to
      the rat's star. You know, shuttle back and forth. A few
      poems remain on the rat's star. Think of rat as a rat, and
      he has a star. I know it's a palindrome but—it's more than
      that, it happens to be the rat owns this star.

from a BBC Third Programme broadcast

[b] ANNE SEXTON

With Mercy for the Greedy

*For my friend, Ruth, who urges me to make an appointment for the Sacrament
of Confession*

Concerning your letter in which you ask
me to call a priest and in which you ask
me to wear The Cross that you enclose;
your own cross,
your dog-bitten cross,
no larger than a thumb,
small and wooden, no thorns, this rose –

I pray to its shadow,
that grey place
where it lies on your letter . . . deep, deep.
I detest my sins and I try to believe
in The Cross. I touch its tender hips, its dark jawed face,
its solid neck, its brown sleep.

True. There is
a beautiful Jesus.
He is frozen to his bones like a chunk of beef.
How desperately he wanted to pull his arms in!
How desperately I touch his vertical and horizontal axes!
But I can't. Need is not quite belief.

All morning long
I have worn
your cross, hung with package string around my throat.
It tapped me lightly as a child's heart might,
tapping secondhand, softly waiting to be born.
Ruth, I cherish the letter you wrote.

My friend, my friend, I was born
doing reference work in sin, and born
confessing it. This is what poems are:
with mercy
for the greedy,
they are the tongue's wrangle,
the world's pottage, the rat's star.

One of the impressive features of *With Mercy for the Greedy* is the
way in which the informality of a reply to a friend is skilfully
suggested by the irregular metre and the phraseology—'con-
cerning your letter . . .' 'my friend . . .'—and yet is given form
and tautness by means of repetition and echo (one of the most
primitive of poetic devices) and a partial, unobtrusive rhyme
scheme. This blend of the personal and the rhetorical is char-
acteristic of Anne Sexton's art. The 'tongue's wrangle' at the
end of the discussion between her and a fellow poet, George
MacBeth, points to the difficulty a poet finds in expressing in
any more abstract terms the meaning that has already been

expressed in an image: 'the rat's star'. Indeed, the antithetical connotations of 'rat' and 'star', fused and yet straining apart, both by their diverse natures and the fact that they form a palindrome, could hardly be improved as an expression of poetry's being at home in a world of sin and splendour.

S: This is a rather cruel poem, you know. It's cruel, my friends say it's cruel, because they say, we who love you hate this poem, because it's so self-destructive, and you are so flamboyant in your addiction. But I say, now wait a minute, although it's about my addiction isn't it true about any addict that they are flamboyant about their addiction, and show it off and say, Look I'm an addict? So it's true about — it's even a—an any-person poem. It's about me, but in truth it must be about any addict, I think.

M: This again, of course, is obviously an autobiographical poem. I want to ask you, though, a question about this. Every act of making a poem is in a certain sense artificial, and even in the most intensely personal poems a certain amount has to be adjusted, to fit the rhythm, or something. Do you feel, when you are dealing with very intense personal experiences, that you sometimes have to compromise at all, sometimes to make it fit metre, sometimes to make it make a poem, to give it a special resonance, and so on?

S: I do, but perhaps not in this poem, although I think it has a universal content. I think that in my other poems I change all sorts of facts, but facts are very unimportnat things. Only make you believe in the emotional content of a poem. If you believe in the emotional content then you know what's going on with the poet. I don't think I've changed—I know I take eight pills and —

M: —they are these colours—

S: —they are these colours, and—they are this beautiful and—and I do think it's—what did I say—'I'm on a diet from death'—I think that's probably the most important thing I say, because it means, instead of killing myself I take the pills. I say these true things—I could have said ten or fifteen pills. I happen to say the truth but it's only happensense, and makes no difference to the truth of the poem, which is that I'm an addict to the pills.

M: This one in fact is really pretty well totally accurate?

S: Yes, it happens to be, but a lot of the autobiographical poems are not accurate—you know, as far as facts go.

M: The other thing is something you mentioned yourself in introducing it, that it has a special kind of flamboyance about it, a gaiety —

S: It is terribly flamboyant, and gay, yes.

M: This special tone, I think, is what makes the poem, in fact.

S: It's what hurts it for the critics.

M: Well, for me it seems to be a poem much stronger because of this apparent, surface cheerfulness. One knows the situation isn't at all like that, but the fact you are able to talk about it like this backs up what you say in lines like 'But remember I don't make too much noise'.

S: That's right, and I *don't* make too much noise. And therefore I'm trying to say, Hello everyone, here is what I do —now watch it, take part in it (which is rather exhibitionistic of me), but remember I don't make too much fuss about the whole bit. I'm very little trouble—is what I would try to say, even about my whole illness I could say this. For after all, I am crazy and I am sick and all that, but I make very little trouble for anyone.

M: This is where I wanted to introduce an idea. It seems to me that your poetry isn't so much autobiographical and confessional as *moral*. That is to say, you are dealing with extreme situations but you're suggesting a way in which one ought to behave in them. In this poem what you're saying is, in fact, that the important thing is when not to cause too much trouble.

S: That's right.

M: You're aware of this fairly consciously are you?

S: No, no, you just brought it up to me.

M: But it comes out.

S: If it comes out that's good. I know that I don't make too much noise, and this is true. And even about my illness I don't make too much noise, but when people are in my presence they're not always aware of illness. They're aware of other factors in my personality which perhaps might be nice, or fun to be with, or something. I mean people say, you're so cheerful how can you want to die, or how can you be a poet, which is the same question anyway. And I can't answer them, because they say, oh well, this is impossible, it can't be you; but it *is* me, it's another side of me.

———

[**b**] ANNE SEXTON

The Addict

Sleepmonger,
deathmonger,
with capsules in my palms each night,
eight at a time from sweet pharmaceutical bottles
I make arrangements for a pint-sized journey.
I'm the queen of this condition.
I'm an expert on making the trip
and now they say I'm an addict.
Now they ask why.
Why!

Don't they know
that I promised to die!
I'm keeping in practice.
I'm merely staying in shape.
The pills are a mother, but better,
every color and as good as sour balls.
I'm on a diet from death.

Yes, I admit
it has gotten to be a bit of a habit—
blows eight at a time, socked in the eye,
hauled away by the pink, the orange,
the green and the white goodnights.
I'm becoming something of a chemical
mixture.
That's it!

My supply
of tablets
has got to last for years and years.
I like them more than I like me.
Stubborn as hell, they won't let go.
It's a kind of marriage.
It's a kind of war
where I plant bombs inside
of myself.

Yes
I try
to kill myself in small amounts,
an innocuous occupation.
Actually I'm hung up on it.
But remember I don't make too much noise.
And frankly no one has to lug me out
And I don't stand there in my winding sheet.
I'm a little buttercup in my yellow nightie
eating my eight loaves in a row
and in a certain order as in
the laying on of hands
or the black sacrament.

It's a ceremony
but like any other sport
it's full of rules.
It's like a musical tennis match where
my mouth keeps catching the ball.
Then I lie on my altar
elevated by the eight chemical kisses.

What a lay me down this is
with two pink, two orange,
two green, two white goodnights.
Fee-fi-fo-fum—
Now I'm borrowed.
Now I'm numb.

'Confessional poet'—a label often attached to Anne Sexton—is misleading. It is true that she commonly, as here, writes out of an admitted personal situation; but she does so not to confess but to make a poem. As she says, the fact that she takes eight pills, etc., is only 'happensense'; what matters is the emotional truth.

Is the poem moral, as George MacBeth suggests? The idea seems to take Anne Sexton by surprise, though she graciously accepts the term. MacBeth's emphasis on the saving grace of her self-deprecatory, witty tone is surely correct. It is healthier to play competitive sport than to go to war; healthier to take sleeping pills than to commit suicide. But perhaps the poem's main impact comes from its depiction, through vivid, deliberately unstable images ('the pills are a mother . . .'; 'where I plant bombs inside / of myself . . .'), of a person's precarious hold on his or her own value. And this is a universal theme, particularly in our age. Is her equation of wanting to die with being a poet merely provocative, or does it contain a truth?

[**a**] from his *Letters*

Friday, 19th March [1819].—This morning I have been reading *The False One*. Shameful to say, I was in bed at ten—I mean, this morning. The 'Blackwood's Reviewers' have committed themselves to a scandalous heresy; they have been putting up Hogg, the Ettrick Shepherd, against Burns: the senseless villains! The Scotch cannot manage themselves at all, they want imagination; and that is why they are so fond of Hogg, who has so little of it. This morning I am in a sort of temper, indolent and supremely careless; I long after a stanza or two of Thomson's *Castle of Indolence*; my passions are all asleep, from my having slumbered till nearly eleven, and weakened the animal fibre all over me, to a delightful sensation, about three degrees on this side of faintness. If I had teeth of pearl, and the breath of lilies, I should call it languor; but, as I am, I must call it laziness. In this state of effeminacy, the fibres of the brain are relaxed, in common with the rest of the body, and to such a happy degree, that pleasure has no show of enticement, and pain no unbearable frown; neither Poetry, nor Ambition, nor Love, have any alertness of countenance; as they pass by me, they seem rather like three figures on a Greek vase, two men and a woman, whom no one but myself could distinguish in their disguisement. This is the only happiness, and is a rare instance of advantage in the body overpowering the mind.

I have this moment received a note from Haslam, in which he writes that he expects the death of his father who has been for some time in a state of insensibility; I shall go to town to-morrow to see him. This is the world; thus we cannot expect to give away many hours to pleasure; circumstances are like clouds, continually gathering and bursting; while we are laughing, the seed of trouble is put into the wide arable land of events; while we are laughing, it sprouts, it grows, and suddenly bears a poisonous fruit, which we must pluck. Even so we have leisure to reason on the misfortunes of our friends: our own touch us too nearly for words. Very few men have ever arrived at a complete disinterestedness of mind; very few have been interested by a pure desire of the benefit of others: in the greater

part of the benefactors of humanity, some meretricious motive
has sullied their greatness, some melodramatic scenery has
fascinated them. From the manner in which I feel Haslam's
misfortune I perceive how far I am from any humble standard
of disinterestedness; yet this feeling ought to be carried to its
highest pitch, as there is no fear of its ever injuring society.
In wild nature, the Hawk would lose his breakfast of robins, and
the Robin his of worms; the Lion must starve as well as the
Swallow. The great part of men sway their way with the same
instinctiveness, the same unwandering eye from their purposes,
the same animal eagerness, as the Hawk: the Hawk wants a
mate, so does the Man: look at them both; they set about it,
and procure one in the same manner; they want both a nest,
and they both set about one in the same manner. The noble
animal, Man, for his amusement, smokes his pipe, the Hawk
balances about the clouds: that is the only difference of their
leisures. This is that which makes the amusement of life to a
speculative mind; I go among the fields, and catch a glimpse
of a stoat or a field-mouse, peeping out of the withered grass;
the creature hath a purpose, and its eyes are bright with it;
I go amongst the buildings of a city, and I see a man hurrying
along—to what?—the creature hath a purpose, and its eyes
are bright with it:—but then, as Wordsworth says, 'We have
all one human heart!' There is an electric fire in human nature,
tending to purify; so that, among these human creatures, there
is continually some birth of new heroism; the pity is, that we
must wonder at it, as we should at finding a pearl in rubbish.
I have no doubt that thousands of people, never heard of, have
had hearts completely disinterested. I can remember but two,
Socrates and Jesus. Their histories evince it. What I heard
Taylor observe with respect to Socrates is true of Jesus: that,
though he transmitted no writing of his own to posterity, we
have his mind, and his sayings, and his greatness, handed down
to us by others. Even here, though I am pursuing the same
instinctive course as the veriest animal you can think of—I am,
however, young, and writing at random, straining after particles
of light in the midst of a great darkness, without knowing the
bearing of any one assertion, of any one opinion—yet, in this
may I not be free from sin? May there not be superior beings,
amused with any graceful, though instinctive, attitude my mind

may fall into, as I am entertained with the alertness of the stoat, or the anxiety of the deer? Though a quarrel in the street is a thing to be hated, the energies displayed in it are fine; the commonest man shows a grace in his quarrel. By a superior Being our reasonings may take the same tone; though erroneous, they may be fine. This is the very thing in which consists Poetry, and if so, it is not so fine a thing as Philosophy, for the same reason that an eagle is not so fine a thing as truth. Give me this credit, do you not think I strive to know myself? Give me this credit, and you will not think, that on my own account I repeat the lines of Milton:

> How charming is divine philosophy,
> Not harsh and crabbed, as dull fools suppose,
> But musical as is Apollo's lute.

No, not for myself, feeling grateful, as I do, to have got into a state of mind to relish them properly. Nothing ever becomes real till it is experienced; even a proverb is no proverb to you till life has illustrated it.

I am afraid that your anxiety for me leads you to fear for the violence of my temperament, continually smothered down: for that reason, I did not intend to have sent you the following Sonnet; but look over the two last pages, and ask yourself if I have not that in me which will bear the buffets of the world. It will be the best comment on my Sonnet; it will show you that it was written with no agony but that of ignorance, with no thirst but that of knowledge, when pushed to the point; though the first steps to it were through my human passions, they went away, and I wrote with my mind, and, perhaps, I must confess, a little bit of my heart.

[Why did I laugh to-night? No voice will tell, etc.]

I went to bed and enjoyed uninterrupted sleep: sane I went to bed, and sane I arose.

———————

Why did I laugh to-night? No voice will tell;
　No God, no Demon of severe response,
Deigns to reply from heaven or from Hell.
　Then to my human heart I turn at once—
Heart, thou and I are here sad and alone;
　I say, why did I laugh? Oh, mortal pain!
O darkness, darkness! ever must I moan,
　To question Heaven and Hell and Heart in vain.
Why did I laugh? I know this Being's lease,
　My fancy to its utmost blisses spreads;
Yet could I on this very midnight cease,
　And the world's gaudy ensigns see in shreds;
Verse, fame and beauty are intense indeed,
But Death intenser—Death is Life's high meed.

The prose passage is from a much interrupted letter-journal to
John Keats's brother, George, in America. He has promised to
copy out poems on the same day they were written. We there-
fore have a unique opportunity to relate the passing ideas and
moods of a poet—at least in so far as he can, or will, express
them to a close relative—with a poem written almost simul-
taneously. The extraordinary tumult of powerful ideas,
memorably expressed; the undercurrent of strain and turbu-
lence; the creative indolence of the morning—all suggest that
one more door of perception has been opened for him. There
is an agonized satisfaction at being a part of this 'rat's star',
earth, in which egoism is as necessary as altruism. Like all
births, this knowledge is a death. The sonnet is the shadow-side
of the letter's exuberance. The letter bursts with vivid images;
the sonnet has very little of his famous and sometimes excessive
sensuousness: the laugh (close to hysteria, surely), and the
heart which he questions, drive out the more familiar Keatsian
beauty. Indeed, the only image external to his own pain, 'gaudy
ensigns', is conventional and jarring. His more characteristic
density ('To load with apples the moss'd cottage-trees') is here
replaced by friction; jagged syntax and rhythms, obsessive
repeats, exclamations and questions, rub the fur of our expecta-
tion up the wrong way, disturbing us, moving us.

[a] from *My Autobiography*

The Land's End is the most sublime thing I have yet seen in nature. How the dark waves dash against those rocks, and foam and hiss, moaning hoarse tales of storms, and shipwrecks, and callous wreckers in days of old! Everlastingly they come and go, smiting the walls of the old cliff with giant fury, and then recoiling in jets of foam! The lighthouse in the midst of the waters, and the sea-birds on the ledges of the rocks, or floating over the waves, or chiming to the hoarse bass of the billows, as they dash through the sparry grottoes,—all conspire to endear it to the memory. The mist is still falling, or rather driving. We are hastening back over the moor, fragrant with flowers, to our nest for the night, ever and anon pulling off a tuft of heather, and asking questions of our cheerful guide, who seems to tell us all he knows. And now the old clock on the top of the stairs is striking eight, Jane is almost exhausted with the day's long journey, and for the *first time in my life* I retire to rest away from home.

. . . When I awoke, the winds were hushed, the mist was gone, the light of the morning was streaming through the window, the sea-birds were wheeling over the down, a robin sang under the eaves of the old inn, and the lighthouse was shining like an angel in the midst of the waters. So away we went in the matin breezes, down, down past Johnson's Head, away on the extreme crags of the Land's End; and, O, what a wilderness of wonders was there! We felt doubly paid for the mist, doubly paid for our long walk, as the huge clouds rolled back from the rising sun, and the great sea became bluer and bluer, and the Scilly Islands rose up to view, and the noisy gulls called to each other in the crevices of the cliff, or cried upon the waters like poets of the billows. I stood upon one of the crags and repeated Charles Wesley's hymn, and felt I had begun a new era in my existence. The Land's End is like a great craggy poem, epic or otherwise. Every poet should read it, and make it his own.

My heart is wounded, and it will not heal:
I pray not that it should; no, let it bleed.
The world is cruel; there's relief in tears;
I pour them out upon the far Land's End.
Methought a spirit wing'd and glistering
In Eden's vesture sat upon the rocks,
And cried, 'All flesh is grass, and like the flower
So fade away the beautiful of earth.
All flesh is grass. The prophets, where are they?
And where the travellers of the mighty past,
Who roam'd among those fearful trumpeters,
And drank the echoes of this mammoth choir? . . .
All flesh is grass.' And the Atlantic waves
Thunder'd the spirit's dirge, 'All flesh is grass.'

John Harris (1820–84) was a self-taught Cornish miner, a kind
of subterranean Clare. He wrote his poems on anything that
came to hand: mallet, thumb-nail, his tinner's hat; and with
blackberry-juice when he could not afford ink. He was able to
leave his native area only three times in his life: once to
Stratford, to visit Shakespeare's birthplace; once to the Lizard
peninsula; and once to Land's End. The two brief visits to the
Cornish coast inspired some of his best poetry, meditative-
descriptive poems in blank verse, *Kynance Cove* and *The Land's
End*. His prose is lush and rambling; but the blend of discipline
and freedom in poetry, and especially in blank verse, gave scope
to rich melodic gifts.

The prose description, part of a letter to a friend written
soon after his visit, gives no hint of the sadness expressed in his
poem. What happened, I think, is that the natural metaphoric
element in poetry has compelled him to stand, facing the abso-
lute emptiness, on his own 'land's end' of loss—the death of a
beloved child, Lucretia.

from her *Journal*

When we were in the woods beyond Gowbarrow Park we saw
a few daffodils close to the water-side. We fancied that the lake
had floated the seeds ashore, and that the little colony had so
sprung up. But as we went along there were more and yet more:
and at last, under the boughs of the trees, we saw that there was
a long belt of them along the shore, about the breadth of a
country turnpike road. I never saw daffodils so beautiful. They
grew among the mossy stones about and about them; some
rested their heads upon these stones as on a pillow for weariness;
and the rest tossed and reeled and danced, and seemed as if they
verily laughed with the wind, that blew upon them over the
lake: they looked so gay, ever glancing, ever changing. This
wind blew directly over the lake to them. There was here and
there a little knot, and a few stragglers a few yards higher up,
but they were so few as not to disturb the simplicity, unity and
life of that one busy highway.

---

[b] WILLIAM WORDSWORTH

Daffodils

I wandered lonely as a cloud
    That floats on high o'er vales and hills,
When all at once I saw a crowd,
    A host, of golden daffodils;
Beside the lake, beneath the trees,
Fluttering and dancing in the breeze.

Continuous as the stars that shine
    And twinkle on the Milky Way,
They stretched in never-ending line
    Along the margin of a bay:
Ten thousand saw I at a glance,
Tossing their heads in sprightly dance.

The waves beside them danced, but they
    Out-did the sparkling waves in glee:
A poet could not but be gay,
    In such a jocund company:
I gazed—and gazed—but little thought
What wealth the show to me had brought:

For oft, when on my couch I lie
    In vacant or in pensive mood,
They flash upon that inward eye
    Which is the bliss of solitude;
And then my heart with pleasure fills,
And dances with the daffodils.

Apart from the commonplace similes of cloud and milky way, there is little in the first three stanzas of *Daffodils* that is not contained in his sister's account. They are practically Dorothy's description versified. But in the fourth stanza, the poet goes beyond the sense experience into a psychic world where transient things are made permanent. We notice, too, a significant difference in pronouns: the journal, with its unegotistical and unobtrusive 'we', is considering the flowers objectively, whereas the poem is relating them to the individual mind. It is tempting, but a little unfair, to say that Wordsworth comes first, the daffodils second, and Dorothy nowhere. However, the brevity of the inward eye's vision, conveyed by 'flash', prevents the poem from becoming too egotistical; the daffodils give of themselves to him only by grace, and unpredictably, at times of apparent idleness—such as Keats described to his brother—when poetry is gestating below the level of consciousness.

[**a**] from his *Journal*

Sept. 6 (1874). With Wm. Kerr, who took me up a hill behind
ours (ours is Mynefyr), a furze-grown and heathy hill, from
which I could look round the whole country, up the valley
towards Ruthin and down to the sea. The cleave in which
Bodfari and Caerwys lie was close below. It was a leaden sky,
braided or roped with cloud, and the earth in dead colours,
grave but distinct. The heights by Snowdon were hidden by the
clouds but not from distance or dimness. The nearer hills, the
other side of the valley, showed a hard and beautifully detached
and glimmering brim against the light, which was lifting there.
All the length of the valley the skyline of the hills was flowingly
written all along upon the sky. A blue bloom, a sort of meal,
seemed to have spread upon the distant south, enclosed by a
basin of hills. Looking all round but most in looking far up the
valley I felt an instress and charm of Wales.

[**b**]   *Hurrahing in Harvest*

Summer ends now; now, barbarous in beauty, the stooks arise
    Around; up above, what wind-walks! what lovely behaviour
    Of silk-sack clouds! has wilder, wilful-wavier
Meal-drift moulded ever and melted across skies?

I walk, I lift up, I lift up heart, eyes,
    Down all that glory in the heavens to glean our Saviour;
    And, éyes, heárt, what looks, what lips yet gave you a
Rapturous love's greeting of realer, of rounder replies?

And the azurous hung hills are his world-wielding shoulder
    Majestic—as a stallion stalwart, very-violet-sweet!—
These things, these things were here and but the beholder
    Wanting; which two when they once meet,
The heart réars wíngs bold and bolder
    And hurls for him, O half hurls earth for him off under
        his feet.

Hurrahing in Harvest is not directly connected with the prose excerpt; they are separated by about three years. But the scenes are sufficiently similar to throw a clear light on the unique qualities of Hopkins' poetry as distinct from his prose. Native to his mind is an intense dwelling upon the individual essence of all things. It has been said of Leonardo that he makes us see the actual air between the artist and the landscape; Hopkins can do the same, in words, both in his poetry and his prose. In his journal entry, we are able to see the Welsh landscape and skyscape almost as clearly as if it had been painted. We see it but do not feel it. The poem, through the energy-thrust of rhythm, rhyme, repetition, and cunning sound-echoes, gives us emotion, not information. How brilliantly, for example, the staccato, gradually unfolding phrases of line 5 pave the way for the unbroken down-rush of the next line. His greatest gift to the poets who came after him was in un-mooring poetry from the Lotus-island of the inevitable iambic pentameter and letting it ride again the ocean of actual, dramatic English speech-rhythms. For all the beauty of alliteration and metaphor that it would retain, such a more sedately Victorian version as this, say—

> 'Wálking, I líft up heárt and eýes, down áll
> That glóry in the héavens to gléan our Sáviour'

—would constitute an enormous loss.

7 JOHN KEATS

[a] from his *Letters*, October 1818

There are many disfigurements to this Lake—not in the way of land or water. No; the two views we have had of it are of the most noble tenderness—they can never fade away—they make one forget the divisions of life; age, youth, poverty and riches; and refine one's sensual vision into a sort of north star which can never cease to be open lidded and stedfast over the wonders of the great Power.

---

[b] *Bright Star*

Bright star, would I were stedfast as thou art—
   Not in lone splendour hung aloft the night
And watching, with eternal lids apart,
   Like nature's patient, sleepless Eremite,
The moving waters at their priestlike task
   Of pure ablution round earth's human shores,
Or gazing on the new soft-fallen mask
   Of snow upon the mountains and the moors—
No—yet still stedfast, still unchangeable,
   Pillow'd upon my fair love's ripening breast,
To feel for ever its soft fall and swell,
   Awake for ever in a sweet unrest,
Still, still to hear her tender-taken breath,
And so live ever—or else swoon to death.

The lake is Windermere, visited by Keats during his tour of Scotland in 1818. *Bright Star* was written soon afterwards. Robert Gittings, in *The Living Year*, has pointed out the close similarity of the star images, and also noted an underlined passage in Keats's folio Shakespeare—Troilus's excited anticipation of consummating his love for Cressida:

I am giddy; expectation whirles me round,
Th'imaginary relish is so sweete
That it inchants my sence: what will it be
When that the watry pallats taste indeede
Loves thrice repured Nectar? Deathe I feare me
Sounding distruction, or some ioy too fine,
Too subtile, potent, and too sharpe in sweetnesse,
For the capacitie of my ruder powers.

Keats has corrected 'sounding' to 'swooning', in his own hand.
Both the general emotion and particular words, 'swooning' and
'death', make it almost certain, as Gittings says, that the poet
had this passage in mind when writing the sonnet. What Keats
read had the intensity of a living experience for him, and the
sonnet is a fine example of a great poet's ability to amalgamate
disparate experiences into one whole. The chasteness of the star
and the sensual bliss envisaged in the sestet are linked only—as
logic dictates—by a negative: 'No.' But deeper than that logic,
the Romantic identification of an absolute sensuous bliss with
death is justified by the image of the star, which, while 'bright'
and 'with eternal lids apart', is whirled inorganic matter.

[**a**] from *Sermon LXVI*

Let me wither and wear out mine age in a discomfortable, in an unwholesome, in a penurious prison, and so pay my debts with my bones, and recompense the wastefulness of my youth, with the beggary of mine age; Let me wither in a spittle under sharp, and foul, and infamous diseases, and so recompense the wantonness of my youth, with that loathsomeness in mine age; yet, if God withdraw not his spiritual blessings, his Grace, his Patience, If I can call my suffering his Doing, my passion his Action, All this that is temporal, is but a caterpillar got into one corner of my garden, but a mildew fallen upon one acre of my Corn; The body of all, the substance of all is safe, as long as the soul is safe. But when I shall trust to that, which we call a good spirit, and God shall deject, and impoverish, and evacuate that spirit, when I shall rely upon a moral constancy, and God shall shake, and enfeeble, and enervate, destroy and demolish that constancy; when I shall think to refresh my self in the serenity and sweet air of a good conscience, and God shall call up the damps and vapours of hell itself, and spread a cloud of diffidence, and an impenetrable crust of desperation upon my conscience; when health shall fly from me, and I shall lay hold upon riches to succour me, and comfort me in my sickness, and riches shall fly from me, and I shall snatch after favour, and good opinion, to comfort me in my poverty; when even this good opinion shall leave me, and calumnies and misinformations shall prevail against me; when I shall need peace, because there is none but thou, O Lord, that should stand for me, and then shall find, that all the wounds that I have, come from thy hand, all the arrows that stick in me, from thy quiver; when I shall see, that because I have given my self to my corrupt nature, thou hast changed thine; and because I am all evil towards thee, therefore thou hast given over being good towards me; when it comes to this height, that the fever is not in the humours, but in the spirits, that mine enemy is not an imaginary enemy, fortune, not a transitory enemy, malice in great persons, but a real, and an irresistible, and an inexorable, and an everlasting enemy, The Lord of Hosts himself, The Almighty God himself, the Almighty God himself only knows the weight of this affliction, and except he put in that *pondus gloriae*, the exceeding weight of an eternal glory, with his own hand, into the other scale, we are weighed down, we are swallowed up, irreparably, irrevocably, irrecoverably, irremediably.

[**b**]   *A Hymn to God the Father*

Wilt thou forgive that sin where I begun,
    Which was my sin, though it were done before?
Wilt thou forgive that sin through which I run,
    And do run still: though still I do deplore?
        When thou hast done, thou hast not done,
            For, I have more.

Wilt thou forgive that sin which I have won
    Others to sin? and, made my sin their door?
Wilt thou forgive that sin which I did shun
    A year, or two: but wallowed in, a score?
        When thou hast done, thou hast not done,
            For I have more.

I have a sin of fear, that when I have spun
    My last thread, I shall perish on the shore;
But swear by thy self, that at my death thy Son
    Shall shine as he shines now, and heretofore;
        And, having done that, Thou hast done,
            I fear no more.

The sermon, preached in his capacity as Dean of St Paul's, and the poem, are from the last years of Donne's life, and they express the same emotion: the ultimate, self-destructive fear that he has 'fallen out of the hands of the living God'. While Donne the poet is clearly present in the sermon—never more so than in the brilliant echo effects of the latinate adjectives and adverbs that climb towards his 'irresistible' climax—it is worth studying the different kinds of rhetoric and tone which the two forms impose on him.

The daring pun on his own name, in the poem, is a profound concentrated metaphor, identifying the fullness of a human life (all that we know as 'Donne') with its extinction ('done'—completed, ended). It is interesting that the other thrice repeated keyword, 'more', evokes the maiden name of his wife, Anne More. There is possibly a buried secondary meaning: 'for I still cling to worldly values, all that is summed in the name More'. Or it may be just a trick of unconscious association. At some stage of writing, the two lines in question became the pivot of the poem; and we can imagine a happy moment when he realized that the whole rhyme scheme could and should follow from the two contrasting sounds.

[a] from *Two on a Tower*

Then they proceeded to scan the sky, roving from planet to star, from single stars to double stars, from double to coloured stars, in the cursory manner of the merely curious. They plunged down to that at other times invisible multitude in the back rows of the celestial theatre: remote layers of constellations whose shapes were new and singular; pretty twinklers which for infinite ages had spent their beams without calling forth from a single earthly poet a single line, or being able to bestow a ray of comfort on a single benighted traveller.

'And to think,' said Lady Constantine, 'that the whole race of shepherds, since the beginning of the world,—even those immortal shepherds who watched near Bethlehem,—should have gone into their graves without knowing that for one star that lighted them in their labours, there were a hundred as good behind trying to do so! . . . I have a feeling for this instrument not unlike the awe I should feel in the presence of a great magician in whom I really believed. Its powers are so enormous, and weird, and fantastical that I should have a personal fear in being with it alone. Music drew an angel down, said the poet: what is that to drawing down worlds!'

'I often experience a kind of fear of the sky after sitting in the observing-chair a long time,' he answered. 'And when I walk home afterwards I also fear it for what I know is there, but cannot see, as one naturally fears the presence of a vast formless something that only reveals a very little of itself. That's partly what I meant by saying that magnitude, which up to a certain point has grandeur, has beyond it ghastliness.'

Thus the interest of their sidereal observations led them on, till the knowledge that scarce any other human vision was travelling within a hundred million miles of their own gave them such a sense of the isolation of that faculty as almost to be a sense of isolation in respect of their whole personality, causing a shudder at its absoluteness. At night, when human discords and harmonies are hushed, in a general sense, for the greater part of twelve hours, there is nothing to moderate the blow with which the infinitely great, the stellar universe, strikes down upon the infinitely little, the mind of the beholder; and this was the case now. Having got closer to immensity than their fellow-creatures, they saw at once its beauty and its frightfulness. They more and more felt the contrast between their own tiny magnitudes and those among which they had recklessly plunged, till they were oppressed with the presence of a vastness they could not cope with even as an idea, and which hung about them like a nightmare.

He stood by her while she observed; she by him when they changed places. Once that Swithin's emancipation from a trammelling body had been effected by the telescope, and he was well away in space, she felt her influence over him diminishing to nothing. He was quite unconscious of his terrestrial neighbourings, and of herself as one of them. It still further reduced her towards unvarnished simplicity in her manner to him.

The silence was broken only by the ticking of the clockwork which gave diurnal motion to the instrument. The stars moved on, the end of the telescope followed, but their tongues stood still. To expect that he was ever voluntarily going to end the pause by speech was apparently futile. She laid her hand upon his arm.

He started, withdrew his eye from the telescope, and brought himself back to the earth by a visible—almost painful—effort.

'Do come out of it,' she coaxed, with a softness in her voice which any man but unpractised Swithin would have felt to be exquisite. 'I feel that I have been so foolish as to put in your hands an instrument to effect my own annihilation. Not a word have you spoken for the last ten minutes.'

'I have been mentally getting on with my great theory. I hope soon to be able to publish it to the world. What, are you going? I will walk with you, Lady Constantine. When will you come again?'

'When your great theory is published to the world.'

Thy shadow, Earth, from Pole to Central Sea,
Now steals along upon the Moon's meek shine
In even monochrome and curving line
Of imperturbable serenity.

How shall I link such sun-cast symmetry
With the torn troubled form I know as thine,
That profile, placid as a brow divine,
With continents of moil and misery?

And can immense Mortality but throw
So small a shade, and Heaven's high human scheme
Be hemmed within the coasts yon arc implies?

Is such the stellar gauge of earthly show,
Nation at war with nation, brains that teem,
Heroes, and women fairer than the skies?

Hardy's emotion, in face of cosmic immensity, has a grandeur which exceeds the power of the episode between Swithin and Lady Constantine, in what he himself described as 'this slightly-built romance', to contain. In *At a Lunar Eclipse*, the same idea and emotion are expressed, but concentrated and clarified. The strictness of the Petrarchan sonnet form, besides providing a fourfold, enclosed, turning and returning effect aptly suited to the theme, makes each word, each rhythm, important. We notice, for example, how in the second, third and fourth lines, alliteration, assonance, the unbroken syntax, and the classical dignity of 'monochrome' and 'imperturbable serenity', create the desired effect of the eclipse's slow and regular encroachment. Secondary meanings and connotations rise to our view after a closer reading; we catch an echo of one of the moon's most famous *maria*, the Sea of Serenity, and the adjective 'meek', so often associated with the infant Jesus, links indirectly with 'Heaven's high human scheme'. Three of the stanzas take the form of questions, heightening the poem's feeling of detachment from terrestrial certainties and absolutes.

[**a**] from *Jude the Obscure*

In the down train that was timed to reach Aldbrickham station about ten o'clock the next evening, a small, pale child's face could be seen in the gloom of a third-class carriage. He had large, frightened eyes, and wore a white woollen cravat, over which a key was suspended round his neck by a piece of common string: the key attracting attention by its occasional shine in the lamplight. In the band of his hat his half-ticket was stuck. His eyes remained mostly fixed on the back of the seat opposite, and never turned to the window even when a station was reached and called. On the other seat were two or three passengers, one of them a working woman who held a basket on her lap, in which was a tabby kitten. The woman opened the cover now and then, whereupon the kitten would put out its head, and indulge in playful antics. At these the fellow-passengers laughed, except the solitary boy bearing the key and ticket, who, regarding the kitten with his saucer eyes, seemed mutely to say: 'All laughing comes from misapprehension. Rightly looked at there is no laughable thing under the sun.'

Occasionally at a stoppage the guard would look into the compartment and say to the boy, 'All right, my man. Your box is safe in the van.' The boy would say, 'Yes,' without animation, would try to smile, and fail.

He was Age masquerading as Juvenility, and doing it so badly that his real self showed through crevices. A ground swell from ancient years of night seemed now and then to lift the child in this his morning-life, when his face took a back view over some great Atlantic of Time, and appeared not to care about what it saw.

When the other travellers closed their eyes, which they did one by one—even the kitten curling itself up in the basket, weary of its too circumscribed play—the boy remained just as before. He then seemed to be doubly awake, like an enslaved and dwarfed Divinity, sitting passive and regarding his companions as if he saw their whole rounded lives rather than their immediate figures.

This was Arabella's boy. With her usual carelessness she had postponed writing to Jude about him till the eve of his landing, when she could absolutely postpone no longer, though she had known for weeks of his approaching arrival, and had, as she truly said, visited Aldbrickham mainly to reveal the boy's existence and his near home-coming to Jude. This very day on which she had received her former husband's answer at some time in the afternoon, the child reached the London Docks, and the family in whose charge he had come, having put him into a cab for Lambeth, and directed the cabman to his mother's house, bade him good-bye, and went their way.

On his arrival at the Three Horns, Arabella had looked him over with an expression that was as good as saying, 'You are very much what I expected you to be,' had given him a good meal, a little money, and, late as it was getting, despatched him to Jude by the next train, wishing her husband Cartlett, who was out, not to see him.

The train reached Aldbrickham, and the boy was deposited on the lonely platform beside his box. The collector took his ticket and, with a meditative sense of the unfitness of things, asked him where he was going by himself at that time of night.

'Going to Spring Street,' said the little one impassively.

'Why, that's a long way from here; a'most out in the country; and the folks will be gone to bed.'

'I've got to go there.'

'You must have a fly for your box.'

'No. I must walk.'

'O well: you'd better leave your box here and send for it. There's a 'bus goes half-way, but you'll have to walk the rest.'

'I am not afraid.'

'Why didn't your friends come to meet 'ee?'

'I suppose they didn't know I was coming.'

'Who is your friends?'

'Mother didn't wish me to say.'

'All I can do, then, is to take charge of this. Now walk as fast as you can.'

Saying nothing further the boy came out into the street, looking round to see that nobody followed or observed him. When he had walked some little distance he asked for the street of his destination. He was told to go straight on quite into the outskirts of the place.

The child fell into a steady mechanical creep which had in it an impersonal quality—the movement of the wave, or of the breeze, or of the cloud. He followed his directions literally, without an inquiring gaze at anything. It could have been seen that the boy's ideas of life were different from those of the local boys. Children begin with detail, and learn up to the general; they begin with the contiguous, and gradually comprehend the universal. The boy seemed to have begun with the generals of life, and never to have concerned himself with the particulars. To him the houses, the willows, the obscure fields beyond, were apparently regarded not as brick residence, pollards, meadows; but as human dwellings in the abstract, vegetation, and the wide dark world.

---

[b]   *Midnight on the Great Western*

In the third-class seat sat the journeying boy,
    And the roof-lamp's oily flame
Played down on his listless form and face,
Bewrapt past knowing to what he was going,
    Or whence he came.

In the band of his hat the journeying boy
    Had a ticket stuck; and a string
Around his neck bore the key of his box,
That twinkled gleams of the lamp's sad beams
    Like a living thing.

What past can be yours, O journeying boy
    Towards a world unknown,
Who calmly, as if incurious quite
On all at stake, can undertake
    This plunge alone?

Knows your soul a sphere, O journeying boy,
    Our rude realms far above,
Whence with spacious vision you mark and mete
This region of sin that you find you in,
    But are not of?

Both the prose and the poem, though impressive in themselves, gain strength from each other's existence. If it were not for the passage in *Jude the Obscure*, we might feel that not enough 'information' had been given us in the poem to sustain the philosophical question of the last stanza. If it were not for the poem, we might find the irruption of this portentous, incurably gloomy boy into the tightly knit exploration of a complex relationship mere bizarre anticlimax. Jude and Sue surely have enough problems without the arrival of 'Little Father Time'! From a formal viewpoint he very nearly wrecks the novel. When his death-wish causes him to hang his foster-parents' two children and then himself, there can be few readers who do not feel that Hardy has pushed his novel over the limits of tragedy into hysteria. And yet—that poem is in our minds. Even if there were not circumstantial evidence that Hardy was reconstructing, remorselessly, his own abandonment of an illegitimate son, we should feel that here was an image of suffering so obsessive, so sharply detailed, that in a curious sense the art does not matter; that the crass, accidental, terrible livingness of life is bursting through the careful arrangements of art. As the sculptor Henry Moore observes, 'there is a fact . . . about the really great artists of the past; in some way their late works become simplified and fragmentary, become imperfect and unfinished. The artists stop caring about beauty and such things, and yet their works get greater.' So with Hardy the novelist, letting loose the nightmarish excesses of reality upon the logic of *Jude the Obscure*, like an ambulance screeching into a calm suburban street. It is likewise arguable that the poem's somewhat stilted style serves to make the central image stand out more searingly, as if no art is hiding the way things *are*. And that is a greater art.

[a] from *Sons and Lovers*

He never forgot seeing her as she lay on the bed, when he was unfastening his collar. First he saw only her beauty, and was blind with it. She had the most beautiful body he had ever imagined. He stood unable to move or speak, looking at her, his face half smiling with wonder. And then he wanted her, but as he went forward to her, her hands lifted in a little pleading movement, and he looked at her face, and stopped. Her big brown eyes were watching him, still and resigned and loving; she lay as if she had given herself up to sacrifice: there was her body for him; but the look at the back of her eyes, like a creature awaiting immolation, arrested him, and all his blood fell back.

'You are sure you want me?' he asked, as if a cold shadow had come over him.

'Yes, quite sure.'

She was very quiet, very calm. She only realized that she was doing something for him. He could hardly bear it. She lay to be sacrificed for him because she loved him so much. And he had to sacrifice her. For a second, he wished he were sexless or dead. Then he shut his eyes again to her, and his blood beat back again.

And afterwards he loved her—loved her to the last fibre of his being. He loved her. But he wanted, somehow, to cry. There was something he could not bear for her sake. He stayed with her till quite late at night. As he rode home he felt that he was finally initiated. He was a youth no longer. But why had he the dull pain in his soul? Why did the thought of death, the after-life, seem so sweet and consoling?

He spent the week with Miriam, and wore her out with his passion before it was gone. He had always, almost wilfully, to put her out of count and act from the brute strength of his own feelings. And he could not do it often, and there remained afterwards always the sense of failure and of death. If he were really with her, he had to put aside himself and his desire. If he would have her, he had to put her aside.

'When I come to you,' he asked her, his eyes dark with pain and shame, 'you don't really want me, do you?'

'Ah yes!' she replied quickly.

He looked at her.

'Nay,' he said.

She began to tremble.

'You see,' she said, taking his face and shutting it out against her shoulder—'you see—as we are—how can I get used to you? It would come all right if we were married.'

He lifted her head and looked at her.

'You mean, now, it is always too much shock?'

'Yes—and—'

'You are always clenched against me.'

She was trembling with agitation.

'You see,' she said, 'I'm not used to the thought—'

'You are lately,' he said.

'But all my life Mother said to me, "There is one thing in marriage that is always dreadful, but you have to bear it." And I believed it.'

'And still believe,' he said.

'No!' she cried hastily. 'I believe, as you do, that loving, even in *that* way, is the high water-mark of living.'

'That doesn't alter the fact that you never *want* it.'

'No,' she said, taking his head in her arms and rocking in despair. 'Don't say so! You don't understand.' She rocked with pain. 'Don't I want your children?'

'But not me.'

'How can you say so? But we must be married to have children—'

'Shall we be married, then? *I* want you to have my children.' He kissed her hand reverently. She pondered sadly, watching him.

'We are too young,' she said at length.

'Twenty-four and twenty-three—'

'Not yet,' she pleaded, as she rocked herself in distress.

'When you will,' he said.

She bowed her head gravely. The tone of hopelessness in which he said these things grieved her deeply. It had always been a failure between them. Tacitly, she acquiesced in what he felt.

Yours is the sullen sorrow,
  The disgrace is also mine;
Your love was intense and thorough,
Mine was the love of a growing flower
  For the sunshine.

You had the power to explore me,
  Blossom me stalk by stalk;
You woke my spirit, you bore me
To consciousness, you gave me the dour
  Awareness—then I suffered a balk.

Body to body I could not
  Love you, although I would.
We kissed, we kissed though we should not.
You yielded, we threw the last cast,
  And it was no good.

You only endured, and it broke
  My craftsman's nerve.
No flesh responded to my stroke;
So I failed to give you the last
  Fine torture you did deserve.

You are shapely, you are adorned
  But opaque and null in the flesh;
Who, had I but pierced with the thorned
Full anguish, perhaps had been cast
  In a lovely illumined mesh

Like a painted window; the best
  Fire passed through your flesh,
Undrossed it, and left it blest
In clean new awareness. But now
  Who shall take you afresh?

Now who will burn you free
  From your body's deadness and dross?
Since the fire has failed in me,
What man will stoop in your flesh to plough
  The shrieking cross?

A mute, nearly beautiful thing
  Is your face, that fills me with shame
As I see it hardening;
I should have been cruel enough to bring
  You through the flame.

The poem is in Lawrence's early conventional style, before he
had found the free verse form that his particular spontaneous
kind of genius required. Metre and rhyme, which in the skilled
hands of, say, Frost or Pasternak, are liberating elements,
reducing the area of chaos from which poems are made, calling
up fresh ideas and images, put Lawrence into a straitjacket.
A rhyme can only work when it appears to be the inevitable
word anyway; in *Last Words to Miriam*, rhyme seems to be
dictating the poem, creating dubious metaphors—'to plough /
The shrieking cross'—and even one crassly artificial grammati-
cal form—'you did deserve'. So too with the metre. 'We kissed,
we kissed though we should not' shows the metre being filled
out by a purposeless repetition; whereas the repetition of 'he
loved her' in paragraph 4 of the prose account is aptly express-
ing Paul Morel's psychological state. Can we say, in fact, that
the prose excerpt is more poetic than the poem?

[**a**] from *Sons and Lovers*

The room was cold, that had been warm for so long. Flowers, bottles, plates, all sick-room litter was taken away; everything was harsh and austere. She lay raised on the bed, the sweep of the sheet from the raised feet was like a clean curve of snow, so silent. She lay like a maiden asleep. With his candle in his hand, he bent over her. She lay like a girl asleep and dreaming of her love. The mouth was a little open, as if wondering from the suffering, but her face was young, her brow clear and white as if life had never touched it. He looked again at the eyebrows, at the small, winsome nose a bit on one side. She was young again. Only the hair as it arched so beautifully from her temples was mixed with silver, and the two simple plaits that lay on her shoulders were filigree of silver and brown. She would wake up. She would lift her eyelids. She was with him still. He bent and kissed her passionately. But there was coldness against his mouth. He bit his lip with horror. Looking at her, he felt he could never, never let her go. No! He stroked the hair from her temples. That, too, was cold. He saw the mouth so dumb and wondering at the hurt. Then he crouched on the floor, whispering to her:

'Mother, mother!'

[**b**]   *The Bride*

My love looks like a girl to-night,
   But she is old.
The plaits that lie along her pillow
   Are not gold,
But threaded with filigree silver,
   And uncanny cold.
She looks like a young maiden, since her brow
   Is smooth and fair;
Her cheeks are very smooth, her eyes are closed,
   She sleeps a rare,
Still, winsome sleep, so still, and so composed.

Like the previous poem and prose passage, we can identify the scene very clearly with Lawrence's own life. *The Bride* seems to me much more successful than *Last Words to Miriam*, in that its form and content are organically related. Perhaps this is partly because the experience is much more immediate and over-whelming, and does not allow Lawrence the gap between the experience and the technique that we sense in the other poem, where we have the impression of a somewhat cold, self-justifying hindsight. The description in the novel is, we may infer, as far as possible a 'total recall' of what he experienced at his mother's deathbed, and it is illuminating to study which elements of the experience he has isolated from the rest, to make a poem.

[**a**] from *Dr Zhivago* (ch. 3)

Pasha, red in the face, his tongue pushing out his cheek, stood in front of the looking-glass struggling with a collar, a stud and the starched buttonhole of his shirt front. He was going to a party. So innocent was he, that Lara embarrassed him by coming in without knocking and finding him with his dressing unfinished. But he at once noticed her agitation. She could hardly keep on her feet. She advanced, pushing the hem of her skirt aside at each step as if it were water she was crossing at a ford.

He hurried towards her. 'What's the matter? What has happened?'

'Sit down beside me. Sit down, don't bother to finish dressing. I'm in a hurry, I must go in a minute. Don't touch my muff. Wait, don't look a second, turn round.'

When he obeyed she took off the jacket of her tailored suit, hung it up and put the revolver in the pocket. Then she went back to the sofa.

'Now you can look. Light a candle and switch off the electricity.'

She was fond of talking in the dark by candlelight and so Pasha always kept a few spare candles. He put a new candle into the holder on the window-sill and lit it. The flame choked and spluttered, shooting off small stars, sharpened to an arrow and steadied. The room filled with soft light. On the window-pane, at the level of the flame, the ice melted leaving a black chink like a peep-hole.

'Listen, Pasha,' said Lara. 'I am in trouble, you must help me. Don't be frightened and don't question me. But don't ever think we can be like other people. You must take this seriously. I am in constant danger. If you love me, if you don't want me to be destroyed, we must not put off our marriage.'

'But that's what I've always wanted,' broke in Pasha. 'I'll marry you any day you like. But tell me plainly what is worrying you. Don't torment me with riddles.'

But Lara evaded his question and changed the subject. They talked a long time about several things which had nothing to do with her distress.

. . .

That winter Yura was preparing an essay on the nervous system of the eye for the University Gold Medal competition. Though he had qualified only in general medicine he had almost a specialist's knowledge of the physiology of sight. His interest in it was in keeping with other sides of his character—his creative gifts and his interest in the relation between imagery in art and the logical structure of ideas.

Just now he and Tonya were driving in a hired sleigh to the Sventitskys'.

After six years of childhood and adolescence spent in the same house they knew everything there was to know about each other and had their own ways and habits, including their way of snorting at each other's jokes and their companionable silences. Now too, they drove almost in silence, thinking their own thoughts, their lips tightly closed against the cold.

Yura was thinking about the date of his competition and that he must work harder at his essay. Then his mind, distracted by the festive, end-of-the-year bustle in the streets, jumped to other things. He had promised Gordon an article on Blok for the mimeographed student paper which he edited; young people in both capitals were mad about Blok, Yura and Gordon particularly. But not even these thoughts held his mind for long.

They drove on, their chins tucked into their collars, rubbing their frozen ears and thinking their own thoughts, but there was one thought which was in both their minds.

The scene at Anna's bedside had transformed them in each other's eyes as if they had only just been granted the gift of sight.

To Yura, his old friend Tonya, until then a part of his life which had always been taken for granted and had never needed explaining, had suddenly become the most inaccessible and complicated being he could imagine. She had become a woman. By a stretch of imagination he could picture himself as an emperor, a hero, a prophet, a conqueror, but not as a woman.

Now that Tonya had taken this supreme and most difficult task on her slender, fragile shoulders (she now seemed to him slender and fragile, though she was a perfectly healthy girl), he was filled with that ardent sympathy and shy wonder which are the beginning of passion.

The change in Tonya's attitude to Yura was equally deep-

It occurred to Yura that perhaps they should not after all

have gone out. He was worried about Anna. They had been on the point of leaving when they heard that she was feeling less well; they had gone in to her, but she had ordered them off to the party as sharply as before. 'What's the weather like now?' she had asked. They had gone to the window to look out, and as they came back the net curtains had clung to Tonya's new dress, trailing after her like a wedding veil. They had all laughed, so immediately striking had been the likeness.

Yura looked round and saw what Lara had seen a little earlier. The unnaturally loud whining of the sleigh on the frozen road aroused an unnaturally long echo from the ice-bound trees of the squares and streets. The lights shining through the frosted windows turned the houses into precious caskets of smoky topaz. Inside them glowed the Christmas life of Moscow, candles burned on trees, guests milled and fooled about in fancy dress, playing hide-and-seek and hunt-the-ring.

It occurred to him that Blok was a manifestation of Christmas in the life and art of modern Russia—Christmas in the life of this northern city, Christmas underneath the starry skies of its modern streets and round the lighted trees in its twentieth-century drawing-rooms. There was no need to write an article on Blok, he thought, all you needed do was to paint a Russian version of a Dutch Adoration of the Magi with snow in it, and wolves and a dark fir forest.

As they drove through Kamerger Street Yura noticed that a candle had melted a patch in the icy crust on one of the windows. Its light seemed to fall into the street as deliberately as a glance, as if the flame were keeping a watch on the passing carriages and waiting for someone.

'A candle burned on the table, a candle burned . . .' he whispered to himself—the confused, formless beginning of a poem; he hoped that it would take shape of itself, but nothing more came to him.

At the end of the day they had a good wash in plenty of hot water and Lara bathed Katya. Feeling blissfully clean Yury sat down at the table before the window, his back to the room where Lara, wrapped in her bath towel and smelling of soap, her hair twisted up into a turban with another Turkish towel, was putting Katya to bed and tucking her up. Enjoying the foretaste of concentrated work, he took in all that was going on around him with a happy, relaxed attentiveness.

It was one in the morning when Lara, who had been pretending, finally went to sleep. Her nightdress and Katya's, like the freshly washed and ironed linen on the beds, shone with lace and cleanliness. Even in those days Lara managed somehow to get starch.

The stillness which surrounded Yury breathed with happiness and life. The lamplight fell softly yellow on the white sheets of paper and gilded the surface of the ink in the inkwell. Outside, the frosty winter night was pale blue. To see it better, Yury stepped into the cold dark room next door and looked out of the window. The light of the full moon bound the snowy plain like white of egg or stiffened whitewash. The splendour of the frosty night was inexpressible. Yury's heart was at peace. He came back into the warm, well-lit room and began to write.

Careful to convey the living movement of his hand in his flowing writing, so that even outwardly it should not lose expression and grow numb and soulless, he set down, gradually improving them and moving further and further away from the original as he made copy after copy, the poems which he remembered best and which had taken the most definite shape in his mind, 'Christmas Star', 'Winter Night' and a number of others close to them in *genre* which later were to be forgotten, lost and never found by anyone.

From these old, completed poems he went on to others which he had begun and left unfinished, getting into their tone of voice and sketching the sequels, though without the slightest hope of finishing them now. Finally he got into his stride and, carried away, he started on a new poem.

After two or three stanzas and several images by which he was himself astonished, his work took possession of him and he experienced the approach of what is called inspiration. At such moments the correlation of the forces controlling the artist is, as it were, stood on its head. The ascendancy is no longer with the artist or the state of mind which he is trying to express, but with language, his instrument of expression. Language, the home and dwelling of beauty and meaning, itself begins to think and speak for man and turns wholly into music, not in the sense of outward, audible sounds but by virtue of the power and momentum of its inward flow. Then, like the current of a mighty river polishing stones and turning wheels by its very movement, the flow of speech creates in passing, by the force of its own laws, rhyme and rhythm and countless other forms and formations, still more important and until now undiscovered, unconsidered and unnamed.

At such moments Yury felt that the main part of his work was not being done by him but by something which was above him and controlling him; the thought and poetry of the world as it was at that moment and as it would be in the future. He was controlled by the next step it was to take in the order of its historical development; and he felt himself to be only the pretext and the pivot setting it in motion.

This feeling relieved him for a time of self-reproach, of dissatisfaction with himself, of the sense of his own nothingness. He looked up, he looked around him.

He saw the two sleeping heads on their snow-white pillows. The purity of their features, and of the clean linen and the clean rooms, and of the night, the snow, the stars, the moon, surged through his heart in a single wave of meaning, and roused in him a joyful sense of the triumphant purity of being.

'Lord! Lord!' he whispered, 'and all this is for me? Why hast Thou given me so much? Why hast Thou admitted me to Thy presence, why allowed me to stray into Thy world, among Thy treasures, under Thy stars and to the feet of my luckless, reckless, uncomplaining love?'

At three in the morning Yury looked up from his papers. He came back from his remote, selfless concentration, home to reality and to himself, happy, strong, peaceful. All at once the stillness of the open country stretching into the distance outside the window was broken by a mournful, dismal sound.

He went into the unlit room next door, but while he had

been working the window had frosted over. He dragged away the roll of carpet which had been pushed against the front door to stop the draught, threw his coat over his shoulders and went out.

He was dazzled by the white flame playing on the shadowless, moonlit snow and could at first see nothing. Then the long, whimpering, deep-bellied baying sounded again, muffled by the distance, and he noticed four long shadows, no thicker than pencil strokes, on the edge of the snow-field just beyond the gully.

The wolves stood in a row, their heads raised and their muzzles pointing towards the house, baying at the moon or at its silver reflection on the windows. But scarcely had Yury realized that they were wolves when they turned and trotted off like dogs, almost as if they could read his thoughts. He lost sight of them before he noticed the direction in which they had vanished.

'That's the last straw!' he thought. 'Is their lair quite close? Perhaps in the gully. And Samdevyatov's horse is in the barn! They must have scented it.'

He decided not to upset Lara for the time being by telling her. Going back, he shut all the doors between the cold rooms and the heated part of the house, pushed rugs and clothes against the cracks to keep out the draughts, and went back to his desk. The lamplight was bright and welcoming as before. But he was no longer in the mood to write. He couldn't settle down. He could think of nothing but wolves and of looming dangers and complications of every kind. Besides, he was tired.

Lara woke up. 'Still at work, my love?' she whispered in a voice heavy with sleep. 'Burning and shining like a candle in the night. Come and sit beside me for a moment. I'll tell you my dream.'

He put out the light.

Snow swept over the earth,
Swept it from end to end.
The candle on the table burned,
The candle burned.

Like swarms of summer midges
Drawn to the flame
The snowflakes
Flocked to the window.

The driven snow drew circles and arrows
On the window pane.
The candle on the table burned,
The candle burned.

On the bright ceiling
Fell the shadows
Of crossed hands, crossed feet,
Crossed fate.

Two shoes fell to the floor
With a thud.
From the night-light
Wax tears dropped on frock.

And everything was lost
In the white-haired, white, snowy darkness.
The candle on the table burned,
The candle burned.

A draught from the corner
Puffed at the candle's flame,
And like an angel, the heat of temptation
Raised two wings in the form of a cross.

The snow swept all through February,
And now and again
The candle on the table burned,
The candle burned.

Lara Guishar is preparing to shoot Komarovsky, her seducer and corrupter. The youthful, idealistic Pasha appears to be her only hope of escape from the corrupt past. Meanwhile Yury Zhivago is passing in the street, his thoughts full of Tonya. Both couples will attain a real and deep union in marriage, but will be forced apart by the Revolution. Yura has already seen Lara briefly; he will see her again at the Christmas party, after her unsuccessful murder attempt. But their union as lovers is far in the future, a consequence of two equally fortuitous, improbable meetings. Later still, Lara is fated to mourn over Yury's body in this same room, in which the candle melted a black chink 'like a peep-hole', and which Yury interpreted as a deliberate glance. A poem takes its confused beginning.

In the second passage we see him revising the poem that came out of that image, *Winter Night*, before beginning to write others and finding himself taken over by a force outside his control. They are in hiding from the sinister impersonal forces threatening them. Lara greets him with a close echo of the poem: 'Burning and shining like a candle in the night'.

The passages are full of interlocked images, principally of light and vision. Yury is studying the physiology of the eye: he is poet *and* doctor; the candle in the room, peep-hole and deliberate glance; Christmas-tree candles; lamplight and moonlight; stars; the shining cleanliness of two pure faces on snow-white pillows; Yura 'looked up, he looked around him'—an action which is echoed constantly in the novel. Sight, most spiritual of senses; and an upward, wide-sweeping look. In Lara's home-town, beautiful caryatid-maidens still support the roof of one of its buildings; though below them, if the glance falls so low, the stone is plastered with vulgar party slogans and proclamations.

A note in Zhivago's journal 'unusual brilliance and coherence of everything', conveys the essence of *Dr Zhivago*. The coherence (rather than coincidence) and the organic flow of life and nature as opposed to machineman's shrill and childish attempt to impose a lifeless process of cause and effect; the coherence and onflow of images which Zhivago experiences so exhilaratingly when writing: this coherence of everything is embodied in the novel, seen as the very element we live in. In its continuously metaphoric use of events, thoughts, phrases of conversation, images, *Doctor Zhivago* seems to me one total, magnificent symbol, with innumerable shades of meaning within the primary meaning, Life. Life, in its Russian form, is the word from which Zhivago derives.

The setting of *Winter Night* is not made explicit. What we are made to feel is that sexual temptation carries with it both pain ('wax tears') and spiritual purity ('the form of a cross'—passion and the Passion). Threatened by chaoses of snow outside, the lovers are consoled by the candle's *burning* (not flickering or glowing), throwing on the ceiling the shadows of their 'crossed fate'.

[a] from *Doctor Zhivago* (ch. 14)

'What have I done? What have I done? I've given her up, renounced her, given her away. I must run after them. Lara! Lara!

'They can't hear. The wind is against me and they are probably talking at the tops of their voices. She has every reason to feel happy, reassured. She has no idea of the trick I've played on her.

'She is thinking, it's wonderful that things have gone so well, they couldn't be better. Her absurd, obstinate Yura has relented at last, thank heavens; we are going to a nice, safe place, where people are more sensible than we are, where you can be sure of law and order. Suppose even, just to be awkward, he doesn't come on to-morrow's train, Komarovsky will send another to fetch him, and he'll join us in no time at all. And at the moment, of course, he's in the stables, hurrying, excited, fumbling with the harness, and he'll rush after us full tilt and catch up with us before we get into the forest.

'That's what she must be thinking. And we didn't even say goodbye properly. I just waved to her and turned back, trying to swallow my pain as if it were a piece of apple stuck in my throat, choking me.'

He stood in the porch, his coat over one shoulder. With his free hand he was clutching the neck of the slender wooden pillar just under the roof as if he meant to strangle it. His whole attention was concentrated on a point in the distance. There a short stretch of the road could be seen climbing uphill, bordered by a few sparse birches. The low rays of the setting sun fell on this open space, and there the sleigh, now hidden in a shallow dip, would become visible at any moment.

'Good-bye, good-bye,' Yury said over and over again mindlessly, as he waited for it, driving the silent words out of his breast into the frosty evening air. 'Good-bye, my only love, my love for ever lost.'

'They're coming, they're coming,' he whispered through dry, blenched lips, as the sleigh shot like an arrow out of the dip, swept past the birches one after another, gradually slowing down, and—O joy!—stopped at the last tree.

His heart thumped with such a wild excitement that his legs were giving way and he felt weak and faint, his whole body soft as cloth like the coat slipping from his shoulder. 'O God, is it Thy will to give her back to me? What can have happened? What is going on out there near the sunset? What can be the meaning of it? Why are they standing still? No. It's finished. They've moved. They're off. She must have stopped for a last look at the house. Or perhaps to make sure that I had left? That I was chasing after them? They've gone.'

With luck, if the sun didn't go down first (he wouldn't see them in the dark), they would flash past once again, for the last time, on the other side of the ravine, across the field where the wolves had howled two nights before.

And now this moment also had come and gone. The dark-red sun still hung, round as a ball, above the blue snowdrifts on the sky-line, and the snowy plain greedily sucked in its juicy pine-apple light, when the sleigh swept into sight and vanished. 'Good-bye, Lara, until we meet in the next world, good-bye, my love, my inexhaustible, everlasting joy. I'll never see you again, I'll never, never see you again.'

It was getting dark. Swiftly the bronze-red patches of sunset on the snow faded and went out. The soft, ashy distance filled with lilac dusk turning to deep mauve, and its smoky haze smudged the fine tracery of the roadside birches lightly hand-drawn on the pink sky, pale as though it had suddenly grown shallow.

Grief had sharpened Yury's vision and quickened his perception a hundredfold. The very air surrounding him seemed unique. The evening breathed compassion like a friendly witness of all that had befallen him. As if there had never been such a dusk before and evening were falling now for the first time in order to console him in his loneliness and bereavement. As if the valley were not always girded by woods growing on the surrounding hills and facing away from the horizon, but the trees had only taken up their places now, rising out of the ground on purpose to offer their condolences.

He almost waved away the tangible beauty of the hour like a crowd of persistent friends, almost said to the lingering after-glow: 'Thank you, thank you, I'll be all right.'

Still standing on the verandah, he turned his face to the

closed door, his back to the world. 'My bright sun has set': something was repeating this inside him, as if to learn it by heart. He had not the strength to say these words out loud.

He went into the house. A double monologue was going on in his mind, two different kinds of monologue, the one dry and businesslike, the other, addressed to Lara, like a river in flood.

'Now I'll go to Moscow,' ran his thoughts. 'The first job is to survive. Not let insomnia get the better of me. Not go to bed at all. Work all through the night till I drop. Yes, and another thing, light the stove in the bedroom at once, not to freeze to-night.'

But there was also another inward conversation. 'I'll stay with you a little, my unforgettable delight, for as long as my arms and my hands and my lips remember you. I'll weep for you so that my lament will be lasting and worthy of you. I'll write your memory into an image of infinite pain and grief. I'll stay here till this is done, then I too will go. This is how I'll trace your image. I'll trace it on paper as the sea, after a fearful storm has churned it up to its foundations, leaves the traces of the strongest, furthest-reaching wave on the shore. Seaweed, shells, pumice, all the lightest debris, all those things of least weight which it could lift from its bed, are cast up in a broken line on the sand. This line endlessly stretching into the distance is the tide's high-water mark. This is how you were cast up in my life, my love, my pride, this is how I'll write of you.'

He came in, locked the door behind him and took off his coat. When he came into the bedroom which Lara had tidied up so well and so carefully that morning, and which her hurried packing had again turned inside out, when he saw the untidy bed and the things thrown about in disorder on the chairs and the floor, he knelt down like a child, leaned his breast against the hard edge of the bedstead, buried his head in the bedclothes and wept freely and bitterly as children do. But not for long. Soon he got up, hastily dried his face, looked round him with tired, absent-minded surprise, got out the bottle of vodka Komarovsky had left, drew the cork, poured half a glassful, added water and snow, and with a relish almost equal in strength to the hopelessness of the tears he had shed, drank long, greedy gulps.

This is the end of me, but you live on.
The wind, crying and complaining,
Rocks the house and the forest,
Not each pine-tree separately
But all the trees together
With the whole boundless distance,
Like the hulls of sailing-ships
Riding at anchor in a bay.
It shakes them not out of mischief,
And not in aimless fury,
But to find for you, out of its grief,
The words of a lullaby.

———————

A few days after the previous episode, their peace is broken by the arrival of Komarovsky, who tells them that their arrest is imminent, and offers them seats on a train to the Far East. Yury refuses for himself, but urges Lara, with her child Katya, to accept. She will not leave without him. Yury agrees to Komarovsky's suggestion that he deceive her by promising to follow.

The reason for his decision is never made clear. He does not seem to know it himself. It is as illogical as Christ's acceptance of the crucifixion; and indeed certain phrases in this episode and the preceding one recall the Passion. We are told, for example, that Yury felt that '*the hour* of his parting with Lara *was at hand*; he would inevitably lose her and with her the will to live and perhaps life itself. He was sick at heart, yet his greatest torment was his impatience for the night, his longing so to express his anguish that others should weep' (my italics). 'Is it Thy will . . .?' and 'It's finished' again recall Calvary. Zhivago's poems return constantly to the Passion and Resurrection. In this episode it could be said that Zhivago resembles Jesus, in his deliberate acceptance of agony; though he is also like Judas, in betraying Lara, by a lie, to her seducer. It is as if, just as he had been in the hands of a greater power when writing poems, he acquiesces to what seems a greater will, that he should give up his love. He is, so to speak, *being written*, and what happens is like one of those images that he might find as a poet— an image astonishing and incredible, yet somehow right. The episode, and the poem, are concerned not with rational choices, but with the need for sacrifice, so that life can grow into new forms: 'This is the end of me, but you live on.' This line also previsions his actual death, when Lara will say, 'Your going, that's the end of me.' In which context, the 'you' who 'live on' is the poetry. Wind is a symbol of inspiration. It is also— echoing Blok—a symbol of the Revolution, out of which at last some good may come.

[a] from *In the Country of the Skin*

But I detest birds, because they cannot kiss. Somehow I had summoned a grave presence of great strength and truth. Dressed in a shift she went to the cupboard and brought out bright cheese. The great table was scrubbed white, and first we ate. Then we loved, where she spread the great white bolsters. She scattered crumbs for the birds. Returning her kindness those birds ate her plums. Grave presence, in that shift among the fruit trees. Great strength and truth treading with bare feet among the waspish cavernous plums. She was cavernous, but not waspish. She and the soft earth swarmed with liquors that felt. Among the trees hanging with ripe fruit, leaf-caverns bloomed and squeezed. The earth was wool-soft between the ancient boulders. Once it was raining and I came up to the garden gate and by the sundial saw an old woman or was it a young one I couldn't tell, until the life of the rain had drenched her to the young skin where the white shift clung. When I first came over the hill, that first night, I had walked too far, I knew nobody, but I had this address, the wife of a former friend. I thought it was the sea, but it was the blue-grey slate roofs gleaming in the hollow. I knocked at the door, she was much smaller than I had expected, she had big hips and an impudent grin, long dark hair, a white shift. She said come in and poured me a glass of straw-coloured wine. There was a big hearth with a fire burning on it, and the smell of timber and stone, like a well. There was a big white wood table, and a recess piled with bolsters and eiderdowns. I was in that house for twelve weeks. Nobody else came. On one side I remember that I was there, and I can still taste the wine and feel the shape of the glass I drank out of that first night. On the other side of things I cannot remember more than the edge of what we did, and I think she told me something I can't get out of my head. She said, I can see this morning you took up a black thread—look! I give you the white, look at me in my shift and take up the white strain. See me in the wet orchard in my shift and you will want me in the black earth, on the soft flower bed with the smell of the soil. She stood in white at the end of the orchard walk and she laughed as she tumbled in the soil and the earth streaked her cheek as she brushed her hair back. She stood at the end of the orchard walk in white like a soft waterfall with caves chuckling. Then I remember that the warm weather came with stubbles of green over the black and we spent days walking over warm turf. I have a picture of a blue flower knocking against a grey stone and the taste of a stalk of grass in my teeth, the turf warm and springy against the length of my body, and her voice saying, no more of this idolatry, do you hear?

―――――

[**b**]   *The Idea of Entropy at Maenporth Beach*

'C'est elle! Noire et pourtant lumineuse'

A boggy wood as full of springs as trees.
Slowly she slipped into the muck.
It was a white dress, she said, and that was not right.
Leathery polished mud, that stank as it split.
It is a smooth white body, she said, and that is not right,
Not quite right; I'll have a smoother,
Slicker body, and my golden hair
Will sprinkle rich goodness everywhere.
So slowly she backed into the mud.

If it were a white dress, she said, with some little black,
Dressed with a little flaw, a smut, some swart
Twinge of ancestry, or if it were all black
Since I am white, but—it's my mistake.
So slowly she slunk, all pleated, into the muck.

The mud spatters with rich seed and ranging pollens.
Black darts up the pleats, black pleats
Lance along the white ones, and she stops
Swaying, cut in half. Is it right, she sobs
As the fat, juicy, incredibly tart muck rises
Round her throat and dims the diamond there?
It is right, so she stretches her white neck back
And takes a deep breath once and a one step back.
Some golden strands afloat pull after her.

55

The mud recoils, lies heavy, queasy, swart.
But then this soft blubber stirs, and quickly she comes up
Dressed like a mound of lickerish earth,
Swiftly ascending in a streaming pat
That grows tall, smooths brimming hips, and steps out
On flowing pillars, darkly draped.
And then the blackness breaks open with blue eyes
Of this black Venus rising helmeted in night
Who as she glides grins brilliantly, and drops
Swatches superb as molasses on her path.

Who is that negress running on the beach
Laughing excitedly with teeth as white
As the white waves kneeling, dazzled, to the sands?
Clapping excitedly the black rooks rise,
Running delightedly in slapping rags
She sprinkles substance, and the small life flies!

She laughs aloud, and bares her teeth again, and cries:
Now that I am all black, and running in my richness
And knowing it a little, I have learnt
It is quite wrong to be all white always;
And knowing it a little, I shall take great care
To keep a little black about me somewhere.
A snotty nostril, a mourning nail will do.
Mud is a good dress, but not the best.
Ah, watch, she runs into the sea. She walks
In streaky white on dazzling sands that stretch
Like the whole world's pursy mud quite purged.
The black rooks coo like doves, new suns beam
From every droplet of the shattering waves,
From every crystal of the shattered rock.
Drenched in the mud, pure white rejoiced,
From this collision were new colours born,
And in their slithering passage to the sea
The shrugged-up riches of deep darkness sang.

Sons and Lovers and *Jude the Obscure* are novels written by novel-
ists who were also poets. *Doctor Zhivago* is some way along the
spectrum towards poetry (quite apart from having its own body

of poems), in that the events narrated, the words spoken, demand to be related to other events and remarks, not simply from a literal, causative point of view, but for their timeless, symbolic connections, 'invisible threads of sympathy'. Yet the narrative has also a naturalism that sets it in the tradition of the novel. *In the Country of the Skin* is much further along that spectrum. We might call it a novel-poem. Reading this extract, which happens to be one of the clearest narrative parts of the book, we are more aware of certain recurring images, such as white and black, plums, wet orchard, shift, and soil, than we are of the narrative. It is a daring attempt to fuse poetry's intuitive vision with the hard reality of character and events, the novel's traditional territory.

The Idea of Entropy at Maenporth Beach was written two or three years before *In the Country of the Skin*; but the similarity of mood and imagery (at least as regards the passage I have selected) makes for an interesting comparison of what is possible in the two forms. The poem's strongly rhythmic pulse can create, for example, more emotional energy; the prose-poetry can combine a denseness of imagery with some of the grit of narrative fact. (See also **37[b]**, p. 141.)

quarry and figure

poems and variations

[a] Manuscript: *Subject for a poem*

Describe Byzantium as it is in the system towards the end of the first Christian millennium. ~~The worn ascetics on the walls contrasted with their (?) splendour. A walking mummy. A spiritual refinement and perfection amid a rigid world. A sigh of wind, autumn leaves in the streets. The divine born amidst natural decay.~~

A walking mummy; flames at the street corners where the soul is purified. Birds of hammered gold singing in the golden trees. In the harbour (dolphins) offering their backs to the wailing dead that they may carry them to paradise. These subjects have been in my head for some time, especially the last.

> When (——) all
> ~~When all that roaring rout of rascals (——) are a bed~~
> ~~When every roaring rascal is a bed~~
> ~~When the last brawler's tumbled into bed,~~
> ~~When the emperor's brawling soldiers are bed~~
> ~~When the last brawler tumbles into bed~~
> When the emperor's brawling soldiers are a bed,
> ~~When the last~~
> ~~When the last~~
> ~~The last robber~~
> ~~The last benighted robber or army fled~~
> ~~When the last~~
> ~~The last robber or his~~
>   thieves' last benighted traveller
> The ~~night thieves' latest victim~~ dead or fled,
>
> ~~Silence fallen~~
>   When
> ~~When starlit purple~~
>   ~~beats down~~
> ~~When death like sleep has destroys the harlot's song~~
> ~~And the great cathedral gong~~
> ~~When~~
> And the silence falls on the cathedral gong
> And the drunken harlot's song

The unpurged images of day recede;
The Emperor's drunken soldiery are abed;
Night resonance recedes, night-walkers' song
After great cathedral gong;
A starlit or a moonlit dome disdains
All that man is,
All mere complexities,
The fury and the mire of human veins.

Before me floats an image, man or shade,
Shade more than man, more image than a shade;
For Hades' bobbin bound in mummy-cloth
May unwind the winding path;
A mouth that has no moisture and no breath
Breathless mouths may summon;
I hail the superhuman;
I call it death-in-life and life-in-death.

Miracle, bird or golden handiwork,
More miracle than bird or handiwork,
Planted on the star-lit golden bough,
Can like the cocks of Hades crow,
Or, by the moon embittered, scorn aloud
In glory of changeless metal
Common bird or petal
And all complexities of mire or blood.

At midnight on the Emperor's pavement flit
Flames that no faggot feeds, nor steel has lit,
Nor storm disturbs, flames begotten of flame,
Where blood-begotten spirits come
And all complexities of fury leave,
Dying into a dance,
An agony of trance,
An agony of flame that cannot singe a sleeve.

Astraddle on the dolphin's mire and blood,
Spirit after spirit! The smithies break the flood,
The golden smithies of the Emperor!
Marbles of the dancing floor
Break bitter furies of complexity,
Those images that yet
Fresh images beget,
That dolphin-torn, that gong-tormented sea.

———————————

Robert Frost said that a poem happens when 'the emotion finds the thought, and the thought finds the words'. This pattern is not universally true. For some poets, the first stage is melodic. The great Russian poet Osip Mandelstam, for example, found the beginnings of a poem in musical cadences in his head, and had practically completed the poem before he sat down to write anything. But Yeats's way of making poetry closely follows Frost's description.

The first passage [a], is the first of fourteen manuscript pages, as transcribed by Jon Stallworthy in *Between the Lines* (Oxford University Press, 1963), which contains a full analysis of the poem's growth. *Byzantium* begins, prosaically, with a 'subject for a poem'. Slowly the poem is hammered out of prose. Very early in the process he imposes upon himself, arbitrarily or rather intuitively, his rhyme scheme (*Between the Lines*, p. 116), one which had served him well in other poems. He seems ready, too, to accept (as a starting point) iambic pentameter; but the first image which opposes eternity to all the brawling life that is to be refined and generalized later into 'soldiery' and 'night-walkers' song'—'Ànd the gréat cathédral góng'—crucially disturbs the pattern. Immediately he will try to extend it to fit the metrical pattern—'And the sílence fálls on the cathédral góng' —but he will prefer the bronze clangour of 'Áfter gréat cathédral góng'. This, in turn, will suggest still shorter lines, thus helping to create the rhythmic variety and subtlety which contribute so much to the passion of the poem. (see also **66,** p. 232.)

[**a**] Manuscript draft for *The Black Tower*

> Say that the men in this old
> ~~goat~~ Lack nothing that a soldier
> ~~Say that the men that keep this~~
>
> ~~Go Towns men & say that the~~ men of the tower
> have got all that
> ~~Have Lack that~~ a soldier needs
> ~~That they lack (   ), & their wine gone sour.~~
> That their (   ) is scarce & their wine gone sour
> And they but feed as the goat herd feeds
> Old tower ~~This desolate spot their home~~
> ~~Here on this spot we stay~~ Oath bound men & we stay
> Not of our kin are they ~~Go for your work is~~
>   ~~Go for your~~ task is done
> ~~Go You are not our kin Was~~ & They say they are not
>   our
>   ~~your~~ kin
>
> You are not of our kin
> That banner comes not in
>   stand
> Our fathers ~~are buried~~ up right in ~~the tomb~~ their tomb
>   But
> ~~Wind~~ Wind comes from the shore
> And they shake when the winds roar
> ~~Among the mountain rocks they shake~~
> Old bones upon the mountain shake
> Old bones shake upon the mountain
>   ~~or among the~~

We thank the towns men in the name of the **Tower**
   it has
Say ~~we have~~ all that soldiers need
Why should it bargain great its power.
Although we feed as the goatherds feed
~~Say to~~
Say
Go to the men of the black pig's banner
   That
~~Say~~ we have all that a soldier needs
      Though is spent & the wine is bitter
~~Though the wine is sour bitter & the bran spent.~~
And we but feed as the goat herds feed
This desolate shore is our home
No talk can make us come

   The (————) our fathers stand up right in the.
~~Old bones upon the mountain~~
   Which ~~the~~ wind comes from the shore
But ~~shake when the wind roars.~~
~~Up from the sea shore.~~
They shake with the winds' roar

                         mountain
~~The old bones shake upon the mountain among the rocks~~
The old bones upon the mountain shake

---

[b]   *The Black Tower*

   Say that the men of the old black tower,
   Though they but feed as the goatherd feeds,
   Their money spent, their wine gone sour,
   Lack nothing that a soldier needs,
   That all are oath-bound men:
   Those banners come not in.

   There in the tomb stand the dead upright,
   But winds come up from the shore:
   They shake when the winds roar,
   Old bones upon the mountain shake.

65

Those banners come to bribe or threaten,
Or whisper that a man's a fool
Who, when his own right king's forgotten,
Cares what king sets up his rule.
If he died long ago
Why do you dread us so?

There in the tomb drops the faint moonlight,
But wind comes up from the shore:
They shake when the winds roar,
Old bones upon the mountain shake.

The tower's old cook that must climb and clamber
Catching small birds in the dew of the morn
When we hale men lie stretched in slumber
Swears that he hears the king's great horn.
But he's a lying hound:
Stand we on guard oath-bound!

There in the tomb the dark grows blacker,
But wind comes up from the shore:
They shake when the winds roar,
Old bones upon the mountain shake.

The Black Tower was written from Yeats's deathbed, in the
South of France, and is dated 21 January 1939—eight days
before he died. For a full examination of its growth and mean-
ing, see again Jon Stallworthy's *Between the Lines.* Passage [a] is
Stallworthy's transcript of a part of an early draft of the first
stanza. The situation is as follows: 'The inmates of a black
tower prefer their present independence to a proffered, and it
may be profitable, alliance to another power not of their kin.
They await the return of someone who died long ago' (*ibid.*,
p. 226). Symbolically, the black tower stands for a dying body;
for Ireland in its relationship to England; for western civiliza-
tion threatened by Nazi barbarism; for a religious belief against
rationalism.

All the elements of the final version are assembled: the ballad-
rhythm and refrain; the imagery; the sentence structure, which
follows the style of a rebuff to emissaries, yet also allows over-

tones of another sense of 'say that . . .'—i.e. '*even if* (we are doomed), *nevertheless* (we shall stand firm).' In the hammering-out, images that are irrelevant to the stoical heroism vanish: 'Towns men', 'desolate spot'. The 'black pig's banner', which refers to a legend that one day Ireland's enemies will be routed in a great battle fought in 'the Valley of the Black Pig', also vanishes, as being too precise and tending to limit the freedom of the symbol. The more self-sufficient the Black Tower can be made, the richer it can become symbolically.

[a] Manuscript draft variants for *The Eve of St Agnes*, stanzas XXIV–XXVI.

XXIV

1–7   A Casement tripple arch'd and diamonded
      With many coloured glass fronted the Moon
In midst w(h)ereof a shi(e)lded scutcheon shed
      High blushing gules; she kneeled saintly down
      And inly prayed for grace and heavenly boon;
The blood red gules fell on her silver cross
      And her white hands devout.

6–8   As is the wing of evening tiger moths
      And in the midst 'mong many heraldries
And dim twilight . . .

XXV

4   Tinging her pious hands together prest . . .
    Tinging with red her hands together prest, . . .
    And rose bloom on her hands together prest . . .

8   [for Porphyro] Lionel.

XXVI

But soon his heart revives—her prayers said
    She lays aside her veil
    She strips her hair of all its wreathed pearl
Unclasps her bosom jewels . . .
    And twists it in one knot upon her head . . .

But soon his heart revives—her praying done
    Of all its wreathed pearl she strips her hair
Unclasps her warmed jewels one by one
    Loosens the boddice from her . . .

    Loosens her bursting boddice . . .
    Loosens her Boddice lace-strings . . .
    Loosens her Boddice, and her bosom bare . . .

Loosens her fragrant boddice and doth bare
Her . . .
But soon his heart revives—her praying done
    Of all its wreathed pearls her hair she strips
Unclasps her warmed jewels one by one
    Loosens her fragrant boddice; and down slips
Her sweet attire . . .
                    to her knees
Her sweet attire falls light
Half hidden like a Syren of the sea
And more melodious . . .
7   She stands awhile in dreamy thought and sees . . .

---

[b] from *Eve of St Agnes*

XXIV

A casement high and triple-arch'd there was,
All garlanded with carven imag'ries
Of fruits, and flowers, and bunches of knot-grass,
And diamonded with panes of quaint device
Innumerable of stains and splendid dyes,
As are the tiger-moth's deep-damask'd wings;
And in the midst, 'mong thousand heraldries,
And twilight saints, and dim emblazonings,
A shielded scutcheon blush'd with blood of queens
      and kings.

XXV

Full on this casement shone the wintry moon,
And threw warm gules on Madeline's fair breast,
As down she knelt for heaven's grace and boon;
Rose-bloom fell on her hands, together prest,
And on her silver cross soft amethyst,
And on her hair a glory, like a saint.
She seem'd a splendid angel, newly drest,
Save wings, for Heaven: Porphyro grew faint:
She knelt, so pure a thing, so free from mortal taint.

69

XXVI

Anon his heart revives; her vespers done,
Of all its wreathèd pearls her hair she frees;
Unclasps her warmèd jewels one by one;
Loosens her fragrant boddice; by degrees
Her rich attire creeps rustling to her knees.
Half-hidden, like a mermaid in sea-weed,
Pensive awhile she dreams awake, and sees,
In fancy, fair St Agnes in her bed,
But dares not look behind, or all the charm is fled.

Keats said that poetry should come as naturally as the leaves
to the trees. That is true. But this also is true—the immense
labour barely hinted at in the neat tabulation of these rejections
in a variorum edition. We see vagueness replaced by precision
and vividness—'Innumerable of stains and splendid dyes' for
'many coloured'; 'vespers' (evening prayer) for 'praying'. Or
we see a documentary reality ('bosom jewels', 'Boddice lace-
strings') replaced by a reality more in keeping with the chastely
erotic tone ('warmed jewels', 'fragrant boddice'). We see the
heavy demands of the Spenserean rhyme scheme being gradu-
ally satisfied—not by compromises with truth, but by using
them, as a mountaineer uses the tackle which burdens him, as
aids to moving closer to the truth of his conception. 'Frees', for
example, is more truthful to the act of unwreathing pearls from
the hair than was his first choice, 'strips'.

[a]   *Bright Star* (?1818)

Bright star! would I were stedfast as thou art!
Not in lone splendour hung amid the night;
Not watching, with eternal lids apart,
Like Nature's devout sleepless Eremite,
The morning waters at their priestlike task
Of pure ablution round earth's human shores;
Or, gazing on the new soft fallen mask
Of snow upon the mountains and the moors:—

No;—yet still stedfast, still unchangeable,
Cheek-pillow'd on my Love's white ripening breast,
To touch, for ever, its warm sink and swell,
Awake, for ever, in a sweet unrest;
To hear, to feel her tender-taken breath,
Half-passionless, and so swoon on to death.

———————

[b]   *Bright Star* (1819)

Bright star, would I were stedfast as thou art—
    Not in lone splendour hung aloft the night
And watching, with eternal lids apart,
    Like nature's patient, sleepless Eremite,
The moving waters at their priestlike task
    Of pure ablution round earth's human shores,
Or gazing on the new soft-fallen mask
    Of snow upon the mountains and the moors—
No—yet still stedfast, still unchangeable,
    Pillow'd upon my fair love's ripening breast,
To feel for ever its soft fall and swell,
    Awake for ever in a sweet unrest,
Still, still to hear her tender-taken breath,
And so live ever—or else swoon to death.

———————

The first version of *Bright Star* is thought by Robert Gittings (*John Keats*, p. 262) to have been written in November 1818, at about the time when he first met Fanny Brawne, his future love, and while his brother Tom was dying of consumption. Its final version was given to Fanny Brawne by April 1819. Gittings observes that the final form is slightly more decorous than the original. I suggest that an ideal version would incorporate some of the changes, but not all.

[a]   'Never pain to tell thy love'

Never [seek *del.*] pain to tell thy love
Love that never told can be;
For the gentle wind does move
Silently, invisibly.

I told my love, I told my love,
I told her all my heart;
Trembling, cold, in ghastly fears—
Ah, she doth depart!

Soon as she was gone from me,
A traveller came by
Silently, invisibly—
[He took her with a sigh *del.*]
O, was no deny!

[b]   'I told my love'

I told my love, I told my love,
I told her all my heart,
Trembling, cold, in ghastly fears—
Ah, she doth depart.

Soon as she was gone from me
A traveller came by
Silently, invisibly—
O, was no deny.

This poem, from Blake's notebook, shows him attempting to refine still further an already very spare and disciplined lyric, by deleting the first verse. Presumably, at a certain stage of composition he saw the opening generalization as a kind of ladder which he could now afford to kick away, since the second and third verses essentially expressed his thought, both concretely enough and mysteriously enough to be effective. The image of the silent invisible traveller, he may have thought, contains such connotations of love, death and spontaneous nature as to make its formative image, the wind, superfluous. However, the poem was not printed in Blake's lifetime, and he may have remained uncertain. Modern editors frequently restore the deleted verse: and incidentally prefer 'seek' to 'pain'. 'Pain' emphasizes the unnaturalness and effort of defining emotion; but its sound is much less in harmony with the rest of the poem.

'Safe in their Alabaster Chambers'
[a] Version of 1859

Safe in their Alabaster Chambers—
Untouched by Morning
And untouched by Noon—
Sleep the meek members of the Resurrection—
Rafter of satin,
And Roof of stone.

Light laughs the breeze
In her Castle above them—
Babbles the Bee in a stolid Ear,
Pipe the Sweet Birds in ignorant cadence—
Ah, what sagacity perished here!

[b] Version of 1861

Safe in their Alabaster Chambers—
Untouched by Morning—
And untouched by Noon—
Lie the meek members of the Resurrection—
Rafter of Satin—and Roof of Stone!

Grand go the Years—in the Crescent—above them—
Worlds scoop their Arcs—
And Firmaments—row—
Diadems—drop—and Doges—surrender—
Soundless as dots—on a disc of Snow—

[c] Edited version

> Safe in their alabaster chambers,
> Untouched by morning
> And untouched by noon,
> Lie the meek members of the resurrection,
> Rafter of satin, and roof of stone!
>
> Grand go the years in the crescent, above them,
> Worlds scoop their arcs,
> And firmaments row,
> Diadems drop, and Doges surrender,
> Soundless as dots on a disc of snow.

———◆———

Such was Emily Dickinson's poetic alienation from her age, and her indifference to fame, that it is as difficult to pin her down to a definitive 'collected poems' as it is for a photograph to pin down the night sky. As with so many hundreds of other poems, 'Safe in their alabaster chambers' never reached a 'final' version, though there is some evidence that the version of 1861 satisfied her more than any of the others. (For the background and full details of the variants, see Thomas H. Johnson's *Collected Poems of Emily Dickinson*, i, 151.)

The first stanza was settled early. Apart from the replacement of 'sleep' by 'lie'—probably a more 'agnostic' word—it does not significantly change through all the many versions. The second was the difficulty. Her friend and sister-in-law, Sue Dickinson, to whom she showed both the versions printed here, suggested that it was, after all, a one-verse poem: 'strange things always go alone—as there is only one Gabriel and one Sun . . .' Emily did not take her advice, but went on searching for that second stanza, divided between the cold, cosmic, majestic imagery of the 1861 version and a more sensuous earth-bound tone.

The third version, **[c]**, is from a modern anthology, with Emily Dickinson's unconventional punctuation regularized. Is it an improvement?

[a]   'I see thee better—in the Dark'

I see thee better—in the Dark—
I do not need a Light—
The Love of Thee—a Prism be—
Excelling Violet—

I see thee better for the Years
That hunch themselves between—
The Miner's Lamp—sufficient be—
To nullify the Mine—

And in the Grave—I see Thee best—
It's little Panels be
Aglow—All ruddy—with the Light
I held so high, for Thee—

What need of Day—
To Those whose Dark—hath so—surpassing Sun—
It deem it be—Continually—
At the Meridian?

——————

[b]   'I see thee clearer for the Grave'

I see thee clearer for the Grave
That took thy face between
No Mirror could illumine thee
Like that impassive stone—

I know thee better for the Act
That made thee first unknown
The stature of the empty nest
Attests the Bird that's gone

——————

The first poem has only one small variant in Thomas H. Johnson's *Complete Poems*, 'pile themselves' for 'hunch themselves'. The second exists only in a transcript made by Sue Dickinson. It looks very much like a variant of the first—and yet it stands in its own right, and its tone is subtly distinguished from that of 'I see thee better—in the Dark'. The latter defines darkness through its opposite, light: ultraviolet, miner's lamp, glowing grave-panels, and sun. The former defines death rather by confronting it unflinchingly: the 'impassive stone' and 'empty nest'; the one 'light' image is not true light, but only a mirror. Classical severity is softened only by the astonishing metaphor of the grave taking 'thy face between'—as though the grave were loving hands.

[a] from *Hyperion*, I. 1–157

Deep in the shady sadness of a vale
Far sunken from the healthy breath of morn,
Far from the fiery noon, and eve's one star,
Sat gray-hair'd Saturn, quiet as a stone,
Still as the silence round about his lair;
Forest on forest hung about his head
Like cloud on cloud. No stir of air was there,
Not so much life as on a summer's day
Robs not one light seed from the feather'd grass,
But where the dead leaf fell, there did it rest.
A stream went voiceless by, still deadened more
By reason of his fallen divinity
Spreading a shade; the Naiad 'mid her reeds
Press'd her cold finger closer to her lips.

Along the margin-sand large foot-marks went,
No further than to where his feet had stray'd,
And slept there since. Upon the sodden ground
His old right hand lay nerveless, listless, dead,
Unsceptred; and his realmless eyes were closed,
While his bow'd head seem'd list'ning to the Earth,
His ancient mother, for some comfort yet.

It seem'd no force could wake him from his place;
But there came one, who with a kindred hand
Touch'd his wide shoulders, after bending low
With reverence, though to one who knew it not.
She was a Goddess of the infant world;
By her in stature the tall Amazon
Had stood a pigmy's height: she would have ta'en
Achilles by the hair and bent his neck,
Or with a finger stay'd Ixion's wheel.
Her face was large as that of Memphian sphinx,
Pedestal'd haply in a palace court,
When sages look'd to Egypt for their lore.
But oh, how unlike marble was that face!
How beautiful, if sorrow had not made

Sorrow more beautiful than Beauty's self.
There was a listening fear in her regard,
As if calamity had but begun;
As if the vanward clouds of evil days
Had spent their malice, and the sullen rear
Was with its stored thunder labouring up.
One hand she press'd upon that aching spot
Where beats the human heart, as if just there,
Though an immortal, she felt cruel pain;
The other upon Saturn's bended neck
She laid, and to the level of his ear
Leaning with parted lips some words she spake
In solemn tenour and deep organ tone—
Some mourning words, which in our feeble tongue
Would come in these like accents (O how frail
To that large utterance of the early Gods!):
'Saturn, look up!—though wherefore, poor old King?
'I have no comfort for thee, no, not one:
'I cannot say, "O wherefore sleepest thou?"
'For heaven is parted from thee, and the earth
'Knows thee not, thus afflicted, for a God;
'And ocean too, with all its solemn noise,
'Has from thy sceptre pass'd; and all the air
'Is emptied of thine hoary majesty.
'Thy thunder, conscious of the new command,
'Rumbles reluctant o'er our fallen house;
'And thy sharp lightning in unpractis'd hands
'Scorches and burns our once serene domain.
'O aching time! O moments big as years!
'All as ye pass swell out the monstrous truth,
'And press it so upon our weary griefs
'That unbelief has not a space to breathe.
'Saturn, sleep on:—O thoughtless, why did I
'Thus violate thy slumbrous solitude?
'Why should I ope thy melancholy eyes?
'Saturn, sleep on! while at thy feet I weep.'

    As when, upon a tranced summer night,
Those green-rob'd senators of mighty woods,
Tall oaks, branch-charmed by the earnest stars,

Dream, and so dream all night without a stir,
Save from one gradual solitary gust
Which comes upon the silence, and dies off,
As if the ebbing air had but one wave;
So came these words and went, the while in tears
She touch'd her fair large forehead to the ground,
Just where her falling hair might be outspread
A soft and silken mat for Saturn's feet.
One moon, with alteration slow, had shed
Her silver seasons four upon the night,
And still these two were postured motionless,
Like natural sculpture in cathedral cavern:
The frozen God still couchant on the earth,
And the sad Goddess weeping at his feet;
Until at length old Saturn lifted up
His faded eyes, and saw his kingdom gone,
And all the gloom and sorrow of the place,
And that fair kneeling Goddess; and then spake,
As with a palsied tongue, and while his beard
Shook horrid with such aspen malady:
'O tender spouse of gold Hyperion,
Thea, I feel thee ere I see thy face;
'Look up, and let me see our doom in it;
'Look up, and tell me if this feeble shape
'Is Saturn's; tell me, if thou hear'st the voice
'Of Saturn; tell me, if this wrinkling brow,
'Naked and bare of its great diadem,
'Peers like the front of Saturn. Who had power
'To make me desolate? whence came the strength?
'How was it nurtur'd to such bursting forth,
'While Fate seem'd strangled in my nervous grasp?
'But it is so; and I am smother'd up,
'And buried from all godlike exercise
'Of influence benign on planets pale,
'Of admonitions to the winds and seas,
'Of peaceful sway above man's harvesting,
'And all those acts which Deity supreme
'Doth ease its heart of love in.
                              I am gone
'Away from my own bosom: I have left

'My strong identity, my real self,
'Somewhere between the throne, and where I sit
'Here on this spot of earth. Search, Thea, search!
'Open thine eyes eterne, and sphere them round
'Upon all space—space starr'd, and lorn of light;
'Space region'd with life-air; and barren void;
'Spaces of fire, and all the yawn of hell.
'Search, Thea, search! and tell me, if thou seest
'A certain shape or shadow, making way
'With wings or chariot fierce to repossess
'A heaven he lost erewhile: it must—it must
'Be of ripe progress: Saturn must be King.
'Yes, there must be a golden victory;
'There must be Gods thrown down, and trumpets blown
'Of triumph calm, and hymns of festival
'Upon the gold clouds metropolitan,
'Voices of soft proclaim, and silver stir
'Of strings in hollow shells; and there shall be
'Beautiful things made new, for the surprise
'Of the sky-children; I will give command:
'Thea! Thea! Thea! where is Saturn?'

    This passion lifted him upon his feet,
And made his hands to struggle in the air,
His Druid locks to shake and ooze with sweat,
His eyes to fever out, his voice to cease.
He stood, and heard not Thea's sobbing deep;
A little time, and then again he snatch'd
Utterance thus: 'But cannot I create?
'Cannot I form? Cannot I fashion forth
'Another world, another universe,
'To overbear and crumble this to naught?
'Where is another chaos? Where?' That word
Found way unto Olympus, and made quake
The rebel three. Thea was startled up,
And in her bearing was a sort of hope,
As thus she quick-voic'd spake, yet full of awe:
'This cheers our fallen house. Come to our friends,
'O Saturn, come away, and give them heart!
'I know the covert, for thence came I hither.'

Thus brief; then with beseeching eyes she went
With backward footing through the shade a space;
He follow'd, and she turn'd to lead the way
Through aged boughs, that yielded like the mist
Which eagles cleave upmounting from their nest.

[**b**] from *The Fall of Hyperion*, I. 216–end

A Dream

Then the tall shade, in drooping linens veil'd,
Spoke out, so much more earnest that her breath
Stirr'd the thin folds of gauze that drooping hung
About a golden censer from her hand
Pendent; and by her voice I knew she shed
Long-treasured tears: 'This temple, sad and lone,
'Is all spar'd from the thunder of a war
'Foughten long since by giant hierarchy
'Against rebellion: this old image here,
'Whose carved features wrinkled as he fell,
'Is Saturn's; I, Moneta, left supreme
'Sole Priestess of this desolation.'
I had no words to answer, for my tongue,
Useless, could find about its roofed home
No syllable of a fit majesty
To make rejoinder to Moneta's mourn.
There was a silence, while the altar's blaze
Was fainting for sweet food. I look'd thereon,
And on the paved floor, where nigh were piled
Faggots of cinnamon, and many heaps
Of other crisped spice-wood—then again
I look'd upon the altar, and its horns
Whiten'd with ashes, and its lang'rous flame,
And then upon the offerings again;
And so by turns—till sad Moneta cried;
'The sacrifice is done, but not the less
'Will I be kind to thee for thy good will.
'My power, which to me is still a curse,

'Shall be to thee a wonder; for the scenes
'Still swooning vivid through my globed brain,
'With an electral changing misery,
'Thou shalt with these dull mortal eyes behold,
'Free from all pain, if wonder pain thee not.'
As near as an immortal's sphered words
Could to a mother's soften, were these last.
But yet I had a terror of her robes,
And chiefly of the veils, that from her brow
Hung pale, and curtain'd her in mysteries,
That made my heart too small to hold its blood.
This saw that Goddess, and with sacred hand
Parted the veils. Then saw I a wan face,
Not pin'd by human sorrows, but bright-blanch'd
By an immortal sickness which kills not.
It works a constant change, which happy death
Can put no end to; deathwards progressing
To no death was that visage; it had past
The lily and the snow; and beyond these
I must not think now, though I saw that face—
But for her eyes I should have fled away.
They held me back, with a benignant light,
Soft mitigated by divinest lids
Half-closed, and visionless entire they seem'd
Of all external things;—they saw me not,
But in blank splendor, beam'd like the mild moon,
Who comforts those she sees not, who knows not
What eyes are upward cast. As I had found
A grain of gold upon a mountain's side,
And twing'd with avarice strain'd out my eyes
To search its sullen entrails rich with ore,
So at the view of sad Moneta's brow,
I ask'd to see what things the hollow brain
Behind environed: what high tragedy
In the dark secret chambers of her skull
Was acting, that could give so dread a stress
To her cold lips, and fill with such a light
Her planetary eyes; and touch her voice
With such a sorrow. 'Shade of Memory!'
Cried I, with act adorant at her feet,

'By all the gloom hung round thy fallen house,
'By this last temple, by the golden age,
'By great Apollo, thy dear Foster Child,
'And by thyself, forlorn Divinity,
'The pale Omega of a withered race,
'Let me behold, according as thou saidst,
'What in thy brain so ferments to and fro!'
No sooner had this conjuration pass'd
My devout lips than side by side we stood
(Like a stunt bramble by a solemn pine),
Deep in the shady sadness of a vale,
Far sunken from the healthy breath of morn,
Far from the fiery noon and eve's one star.
Onward I look'd beneath the gloomy boughs,
And saw, what first I thought an image huge,
Like to the image pedestal'd so high
In Saturn's temple. Then Moneta's voice
Came brief upon mine ear—'So Saturn sat
When he had lost his Realms'—Whereon there grew
A power within me of enormous ken
To see as a god sees, and take the depth
Of things as nimbly as the outward eye
Can size and shape pervade. The lofty theme
At those few words hung vast before my mind,
With half-unravel'd web. I set myself
Upon an eagle's watch, that I might see,
And seeing ne'er forget. No stir of life
Was in this shrouded vale, not so much air
As in the zoning of a summer's day
Robs not one light seed from the feather'd grass,
But where the dead leaf fell there did it rest.
A stream went voiceless by, still deaden'd more
By reason of the fallen Divinity
Spreading more shade; the Naiad 'mid her reeds
Prest her cold finger closer to her lips.
Along the margin-sand large footmarks went
No farther that to where old Saturn's feet
Had rested, and there slept—how long a sleep!
Degraded, cold, upon the sodden ground
His old right hand lay nerveless, listless, dead,

Unsceptred; and his realmless eyes were clos'd,
While his bow'd head seem'd listening to the Earth,
His ancient mother, for some comfort yet.

It seem'd no force could wake him from his place;
But there came one who, with a kindred hand,
Touch'd his wide shoulders after bending low
With reverence, though to one who knew it not.
Then came the griev'd voice of Mnemosyne,
And griev'd I hearken'd. 'That Divinity
'Whom thou saw'st step from yon forlornest wood,
'And with slow pace approach our fallen King,
'Is Thea, softest-natur'd of our Brood.'
I mark'd the Goddess in fair statuary
Surpassing wan Moneta by the head,
And in her sorrow nearer woman's tears.
There was a listening fear in her regard,
As if calamity had but begun;
As if the vanward clouds of evil days
Had spent their malice, and the sullen rear
Was with its stored thunder labouring up.
One hand she press'd upon that aching spot
Where beats the human heart, as if just there,
Though an immortal, she felt cruel pain;
The other upon Saturn's bended neck
She laid, and to the level of his hollow ear,
Leaning with parted lips, some words she spake
In solemn tenor and deep organ tune—
Some mourning words, which in our feeble tongue
Would come in this-like accenting (how frail
To that large utterance of the early Gods!):
'Saturn! look up—and for what, poor lost King?
'I have no comfort for thee; no not one;
'I cannot cry, *Wherefore thus sleepest thou?*
'For Heaven is parted from thee, and the Earth
'Knows thee not, so afflicted, for a God;
'And Ocean too, with all its solemn noise,
'Has from thy sceptre pass'd, and all the air
'Is emptied of thine hoary majesty.
'Thy thunder, captious at the new command,

86

'Rumbles reluctant o'er our fallen house;
'And thy sharp lightning, in unpractised hands,
'Scorches and burns our once serene domain.
'With such remorseless speed still come new woes,
'That unbelief has not a space to breathe.
'Saturn! sleep on. Me thoughtless, why should I
'Thus violate thy slumbrous solitude?
'Why should I ope thy melancholy eyes?
'Saturn, sleep on, while at thy feet I weep.'

   As when upon a tranced summer night
Forests, branch-charmed by the earnest stars,
Dream, and so dream all night, without a noise,
Save from one gradual solitary gust,
Swelling upon the silence; dying off;
As if the ebbing air had but one wave;
So came these words, and went; the while in tears
She prest her fair large forehead to the earth,
Just where her fallen hair might spread in curls,
A soft and silken mat for Saturn's feet.
Long, long these two were postured motionless,
Like sculpture builded-up upon the grave
Of their own power. A long awful time
I look'd upon them: still they were the same;
The frozen God still bending to the earth,
And the sad Goddess weeping at his feet,
Moneta silent. Without stay or prop,
But my own weak mortality, I bore
The load of this eternal quietude,
The unchanging gloom, and the three fixed shapes
Ponderous upon my senses, a whole moon.
For by my burning brain I measured sure
Her silver seasons shedded on the night,
And every day by day methought I grew
More gaunt and ghostly. Oftentimes I pray'd
Intense, that Death would take me from the Vale
And all its burthens. Gasping with despair
Of change, hour after hour I curs'd myself;
Until old Saturn rais'd his faded eyes,
And look'd around and saw his kingdom gone,

And all the gloom and sorrow of the place,
And that fair kneeling Goddess at his feet.
As the moist scent of flowers and grass and leaves
Fills forest dells with a pervading air,
Known to the woodland nostril, so the words
Of Saturn fill'd the mossy glooms around,
Even to the hollows of time-eaten oaks,
And to the windings of the foxes' hole,
With sad low tones, while thus he spake, and sent
Strange musings to the solitary Pan!
'Moan, brethren, moan; for we are swallow'd up
'And buried from all Godlike exercise
'Of influence benign on planets pale,
'And peaceful sway above man's harvesting,
'And all those acts which Deity supreme
'Doth ease its heart of love in. Moan and wail.
'Moan, brethren, moan; for lo, the rebel spheres
'Spin round, the stars their ancient courses keep,
'Clouds still with shadowy moisture haunt the earth,
'Still suck their fill of light from sun and moon;
'Still buds the tree, and still the sea-shores murmur.
'There is no death in all the Universe,
'No smell of death—there shall be death. Moan, moan,
'Moan, Cybele, moan; for thy pernicious Babes
'Have changed a god into an aching Palsy.
'Moan, brethren, moan, for I have no strength left,
'Weak as the reed—weak—feeble as my voice—
'O, O, the pain, the pain of feebleness.
'Moan, moan, for still I thaw—or give me help;
'Throw down those imps, and give me victory.
'Let me hear other groans, and trumpets blown
'Of triumph calm, and hymns of festival
'From the gold peaks of Heaven's high-piled clouds—
'Voices of soft proclaim, and silver stir
'Of strings in hollow shells. And there shall be
'Beautiful things made new for the surprise
'Of the sky-children.' So he feebly ceas'd,
With such a poor and sickly sounding pause,
Methought I heard some old man of the earth
Bewailing earthly loss; nor could my eyes

And ears act with that pleasant unison of sense
Which marries sweet sound with the grace of form,
And dolorous accent from a tragic harp
With large-limb'd visions. More I scrutinized:
Still fix'd he sat beneath the sable trees,
Whose arms spread straggling in wild serpent forms,
With leaves all hush'd; his awful presence there
(Now all was silent) gave a deadly lie
To what I erewhile heard; only his lips
Trembled amid the white curls of his beard.
They told the truth, though, round, the snowy locks
Hung nobly, as upon the face of heaven
A mid-day fleece of clouds. Thea arose,
And stretched her white arm through the hollow dark,
Pointing somewhither: whereat he too rose
Like a vast giant, seen by men at sea
To grow pale from the waves at dull midnight.
They melted from my sight into the woods;
Ere I could turn, Moneta cried, 'These twain
'Are speeding to the families of grief,
'Where roof'd in by black rocks they waste, in pain
'And darkness, for no hope.' And she spake on,
As ye may read who can unwearied pass
Onward from th'Antichamber of this dream,
Where even at the open doors awhile
I must delay, and glean my memory
Of her high phrase—perhaps no further dare.

There is, in a sense, one poem of inexhaustible forms that is
written afresh in every age. It could be called the poem of
rebirth, of moving through chaos and death into individuation.
Dante's *Divine Comedy*, Milton's *Paradise Lost*, and Pasternak's
Doctor Zhivago, are, in a sense, the same poem but with a
different form to suit its age's spirit. It is not for nothing that the
poets who make this poem approach their task with a special
feeling of reverence and of submission to a power greater than
they; see themselves as mediating the poem rather than making
it.

For Keats, who grew so quickly from callowness into poetry, love and death, the poem took the form, not of a Catholic or Protestant epic, nor of a poem-novel about historical necessity, but of an epic concerning the Greek myth of the destruction of the Titans and the rise of new gods; among them, pre-eminently, the poet-god Apollo. At the beginning and the end of the single 'marvellous year' granted him—Autumn 1818 to Autumn 1819—he attempted the rebirth poem; but each time left it a fragment. By the time he came to take up *Hyperion*, he was no longer content to let the remote gods endure the suffering: he, John Keats, must burn through it, guided by Moneta, the Goddess of Knowledge, a presence as awesome as death itself.

To study the way he has fused the classical, objective *Hyperion* and the personal 'Dream' is a moving and rewarding experience. If, in the end, the difficulties proved insuperable, we should only be disappointed if we believed that this poem can ever be *finally* written. 'Art', said Dr Zhivago, 'is always meditating upon death, and thereby always creating life.'

[a] from *The Prelude* (1805), XI. 279–343

                         At a time
When scarcely (I was then not six years old)
My hand could hold a bridle, with proud hopes
I mounted, and we rode towards the hills:
We were a pair of horsemen; honest James
Was with me, my encourager and guide.
We had not travell'd long, ere some mischance
Disjoin'd me from my Comrade, and, through fear
Dismounting, down the rough and stony Moor
I led my Horse, and stumbling on, at length
Came to a bottom, where in former times
A Murderer had been hung in iron chains.
The Gibbet-mast was moulder'd down, the bones
And iron case were gone; but on the turf,
Hard by, soon after that fell deed was wrought
Some unknown hand had carved the Murderer's name.
The monumental writing was engraven
In times long past, and still, from year to year,
By superstition of the neighbourhood,
The grass is clear'd away; and to this hour
The letters are all fresh and visible.
Faltering, and ignorant where I was, at length
I chanced to espy those characters inscribed
On the green sod: forthwith I left the spot
And, reascending the bare Common, saw
A naked Pool that lay beneath the hills,
The Beacon on the summit, and more near,
A girl who bore a Pitcher on her head
And seem'd with difficult steps to force her way
Against the blowing wind. It was, in truth,
An ordinary sight; but I should need
Colours and words that are unknown to man
To paint the visionary dreariness
Which, while I look'd all round for my lost guide,
Did at that time invest the naked Pool,
The Beacon on the lonely Eminence,

The Woman, and her garments vex'd and toss'd
By the strong wind. When, in a blessed season
With those two dear Ones, to my heart so dear,
When in the blessed time of early love,
Long afterwards, I roam'd about
In daily presence of this very scene,
Upon the naked pool and dreary crags,
And on the melancholy Beacon, fell
The spirit of pleasure and youth's golden gleam;
And think ye not with radiance more divine
From these remembrances, and from the power
They left behind? So feeling comes in aid
Of feeling, and diversity of strength
Attends us, if but once we have been strong.
Oh! mystery of Man, from what a depth
Proceed thy honours! I am lost, but see
In simple childhood something of the base
On which thy greatness stands, but this I feel,
That from thyself it is that thou must give,
Else never canst receive. The days gone by
Come back upon me from the dawn almost
Of life: the hiding-places of my power
Seem open; I approach, and then they close;
I see by glimpses now; when age comes on,
May scarcely see at all, and I would give,
While yet we may, as far as words can give,
A substance and a life to what I feel:
I would enshrine the spirit of the past
For future restoration.

———————

[b] from *The Prelude* (1850), XII. 225–286

                              I remember well,
That once, while yet my inexperienced hand
Could scarcely hold a bridle, with proud hopes
I mounted, and we journeyed towards the hills:
An ancient servant of my father's house
Was with me, my encourager and guide:

We had not travelled long, ere some mischance
Disjoined me from my comrade; and, through fear
Dismounting, down the rough and stony moor
I led my horse, and, stumbling on, at length
Came to a bottom, where in former times
A murderer had been hung in iron chains.
The gibbet-mast had mouldered down, the bones
And iron case were gone; but on the turf,
Hard by, soon after that fell deed was wrought,
Some unknown hand had carved the murderer's name.
The monumental letters were inscribed
In times long past; but still, from year to year,
By superstition of the neighbourhood,
The grass is cleared away, and to this hour
The characters are fresh and visible:
A casual glance had shown them, and I fled,
Faltering and faint, and ignorant of the road:
Then, reascending the bare common, saw
A naked pool that lay beneath the hills,
The beacon on the summit, and, more near,
A girl, who bore a pitcher on her head,
And seemed with difficult steps to force her way
Against the blowing wind. It was, in truth,
An ordinary sight; but I should need
Colours and words that are unknown to man,
To paint the visionary dreariness
Which, while I looked all round for my lost guide,
Invested moorland waste, and naked pool,
The beacon crowning the lone eminence,
The female and her garments vexed and tossed
By the strong wind. When, in the blessèd hours
Of early love, the loved one at my side,
I roamed, in daily presence of this scene,
Upon the naked pool and dreary crags,
And on the melancholy beacon, fell
A spirit of pleasure and youth's golden gleam;
And think ye not with radiance more sublime
For these remembrances, and for the power
They had left behind? So feeling comes in aid
Of feeling, and diversity of strength

Attends us, if but once we have been strong.
Oh! mystery of man, from what a depth
Proceed thy honours. I am lost, but see
In simple childhood something of the base
On which thy greatness stands; but this I feel,
That from thyself it comes, that thou must give,
Else never canst receive. The days gone by
Return upon me almost from the dawn
Of life; the hiding-places of man's power
Open; I would approach them, but they close.
I see by glimpses now; when age comes on,
May scarcely see at all; and I would give,
While yet we may, as far as words can give,
Substance and life to what I feel, enshrining,
Such is my hope, the spirit of the Past
For future restoration.

The Prelude was essentially completed by 1805, but not published until 1850. In his old age Wordsworth carefully revised the great autobiographical poem of his prime. This passage, for example, shows him trying to make his style tauter; and we should not assume that, because Wordsworth's creative powers had withdrawn, the changes must be for the worse. The most striking emendation—'Woman' into 'female'—has divided the critics. Ernest de Selincourt, who was responsible for the first publication of the original version in 1926, found the change 'hard to forgive'. Others see it as a stroke of genius. The point at issue is whether the context requires a more, or a less, personalized word.

[a] from *The Rubáiyát of Omar Khayyám* (1859)

Awake! for Morning in the Bowl of Night
Has flung the Stone that puts the Stars to Flight:
   And Lo! the Hunter of the East has caught
The Sultan's Turret in a Noose of Light

Dreaming when Dawn's Left Hand was in the Sky
I heard a Voice within the Tavern cry,
   'Awake, my Little ones, and fill the Cup
Before Life's Liquor in its Cup be dry.'

And, as the Cock crew, those who stood before
The Tavern shouted—'Open then the Door!
   You know how little while we have to stay,
And, once departed, may return no more.'

. . .

Here with a Loaf of Bread beneath the Bough,
A Flask of Wine, a Book of Verse—and Thou
   Beside me singing in the Wilderness—
And Wilderness is Paradise enow.

'How sweet is mortal Sovranty!'—think some:
Others—'How blest the Paradise to come!'
   Ah, take the Cash in hand and waive the Rest;
Oh, the brave Music of a *distant* Drum!

Look to the Rose that blows about us—'Lo,
Laughing,' she says, 'into the World I blow:
   At once the silken Tassel of my Purse
Tear, and its Treasure on the Garden throw.'

. . .

Ah Love! could thou and I with Fate conspire
To grasp this sorry Scheme of Things entire,
   Would not we shatter it to bits—and then
Re-mould it nearer to the Heart's Desire!

Ah, Moon of my Delight, who know'st no wane,
The Moon of Heav'n is rising once again:
    How oft hereafter rising shall she look
Through this same Garden after me—in vain!

And when Thyself with shining Foot shall pass
Among the Guests Star-scatter'd on the Grass,
    And in thy joyous Errand reach the Spot
Where I made one—turn down an empty Glass!

***

[**b**] from *The Rubáiyát of Omar Khayyám* (1868)

Wake! For the Sun behind yon Eastern height
Has chased the Session of the Stars from Night;
    And, to the field of Heav'n ascending, strikes
The Sultan's Turret with a Shaft of Light.

Before the phantom of False morning died,
Methought a Voice within the Tavern cried,
    'When all the Temple is prepared within,
Why lags the drowsy Worshipper outside?'

And, as the Cock crew, those who stood before
The Tavern shouted—'Open then the door!
    You know how little while we have to stay,
And, once departed, may return no more.'

. . .

Here with a little Bread beneath the Bough,
A Flask of Wine, a Book of Verse—and Thou
    Beside me singing in the Wilderness—
Oh, wilderness were Paradise enow!

Some for the Glories of This World; and some
Sigh for the Prophet's Paradise to come;
    Ah, take the Cash, and let the Promise go,
Nor heed the music of a distant Drum!

96

Were it not Folly, Spider-like to spin
The Thread of present Life away to win—
   What? for ourselves, who know not if we shall
Breathe out the very Breath we now breathe in!

Look to the blowing Rose about us—'Lo,
Laughing,' she says, 'into the world I blow:
   At once the silken tassel of my Purse
Tear, and its Treasure on the Garden throw.'

. . .

Ah Love! could you and I with Fate conspire
To grasp this sorry Scheme of Things entire,
   Would not we shatter it to bits—and then
Re-mould it nearer to the Heart's Desire!

But see! The rising Moon of Heav'n again
Looks for us, Sweet-heart, through the quivering Plane:
   How oft hereafter rising will she look
Among those leaves—for one of us in vain!

And when Yourself with silver Foot shall pass
Among the Guests Star-scatter'd on the Grass,
   And in your joyous errand reach the spot
Where I made One—turn down an empty Glass!

A brilliant foreshadower of Robert Lowell's 'imitations' (see
31[b], p. 120), Fitzgerald's *Rubáiyát* lives on in its first version,
not its second. Except when a poem haunts its author's mind
because it has not fully embodied his vision, long-delayed
second bites at the cherry are rarely successful. The balance
between passion and logic is disturbed in favour of the latter;
so that there is a temptation to be too clever—'the quivering
Plane'—too explanatory—'False Morning'—and too cautious
—the disappearance of 'Ah! Moon of my Delight' turns the
penultimate verse into a sentimental Victorian love-song.

[a] Variant 1

The Unquiet Grave

Cold blows the wind tonight, sweetheart,
Cold are the drops of rain.
The very first love that ever I had
In greenwood he was slain.

I'll do as much for my true love
As any young woman may.
I'll sit and mourn above his grave
A twelvemonth and a day.

A twelvemonth and a day being up
The ghost began to speak.
Why sit you here by my graveside
And will not let me sleep?

O think upon the garden, love,
Where you and I did walk.
The fairest flower that blossomed there
Is withered on the stalk.

The stalk will bear no leaves, sweetheart,
The flowers will never return,
And my true love is dead, is dead,
And I do nought but mourn.

What is it that you want of me
And will not let me sleep?
Your salten tears they trickle down
And wet my winding sheet.

What is it that I want of thee,
O what of thee in thy grave?
A kiss from off thy clay cold lips,
And that is all I crave.

Cold are my lips in death, sweetheart,
My breath is earthy strong.
If you do touch my clay cold lips
Your time will not be long.

Cold though your lips in death, sweetheart,
One kiss is all I crave.
I care not, if I kiss but thee,
That I should share thy grave.

Go fetch me a light from dungeon deep,
Wring water from a stone,
And likewise milk from a maiden's breast
Which never babe had none.

She stroke a light from out a flint,
An ice-bell pressèd she,
She pressed the milk from a Johnnis wort
And so she did all three.

Now if you were not true in word
As now I know you be
I'd tear you as the withered leaves
Are torn from off the tree.

Now I have mourned upon his grave
A twelve month and a day,
I'll set my sail before the wind
To waft me far away.

——————

[b] Variant 2

So cold the wintry winds do blow
And down fell drops of rain.
I have had but one true love,
In greenwood she was slain.

I'll say as much for my true love
As any young man could say.
I'll sit and I'll weep on her cold grave
For a twelve month and a day.

When the twelve month and a day was up
The ghost began to weep.
Why do you sit here on my grave
And will not let me sleep?

There's one thing more that I do want
And that is all I crave,
And that is to kiss your lily-white lips
And I will go from your grave.

My lips they are as cold as clay,
My breath smells heavy and strong,
And if you kiss my lily-white lips
Your time will not be long.

Down in the garden of myrtle green
Where my true love and me did walk
The finest flower that ever was seen
Is withered unto the stalk.

The stalk is withered unto the root
And the root unto the ground.
That's why I mourn for the loss of my love
When she's not here to be found.

———

Like all the best oral poetry, *The Unquiet Grave* is drawn up to us
out of a measureless well of experience: our need to mourn and
yet, at the right time, to dance over the bones. There is an
interesting American Indian parallel; in the words of a Zuñi
widow: 'For one year I would cry. I was thoughtful for my old
husband. Then father spoke with me. Then I was happy. I did
not worry. My uncle desired it for me. "It is all right, niece.
Do not cry. It cannot be helped. It is ever thus. Do not think
of where you have come from, but rather look forward to
where you are to go . . ." ' (Ruth Bunzel: *Zuñi Texts*).

These two, out of many extant versions, are quoted as (A)
and (B) in James Reeves's *The Everlasting Circle* (p. 272). A third
variant can be found in Part IV, **52[a]**. Reeves suggests that
stanzas 10 and 11 of (A), the lover's tasks, are extraneous; but
also that all the variants where not actually confused, are
perhaps fragments of a longer, undiscovered original.

Is it possible and legitimate for us to evolve a single poem,
incorporating the best elements of all the variants? Or does the
strength of oral poems partly depend upon their having the
rough edges of human imperfection?

[a] from *Macbeth*, V.iii.19–28

MACBETH: Take thy face hence. [*Exit Servant.*]—Seyton!—I am
    sick at heart,
When I behold—Seyton, I say!—This push
Will cheer me ever, or disseat me now.
I have liv'd long enough: my way of life
Is fall'n into the sere, the yellow leaf;
And that which should accompany old age,
As honour, love, obedience, troops of friends,
I must not look to have; but in their stead,
Curses, not loud, but deep, mouth-honour, breath,
Which the poor heart would fain deny, and dare not.

———

[b] The same: Samuel Johnson's conjectural reading

MACBETH: Take thy face hence. [*Exit Servant*].—Seyton!—I am
    sick at heart,
When I behold—Seyton, I say!—This push
Will chair me ever, or disseat me now.
I have liv'd long enough: my May of life
Is fall'n into the sere, the yellow leaf;
And that which should accompany old age,
As honour, love, obedience, troops of friends,
I must not look to have; but in their stead,
Curses, not loud, but deep, mouth-honour, breath,
Which the poor heart would fain deny, and dare not.

To the urbane eighteenth-century mind, Shakespeare's genius appeared too wild and disordered. Dr Johnson conjectured 'May' instead of the Folio's 'way' because he could see no connection between the latter and the succeeding image of autumn. But it is possible for a metaphor to be too carefully followed through, especially when some extreme emotion is being expressed in dialogue. Furthermore, is Macbeth more likely to be thinking of a particular period of his life (his youth) or of the whole pattern and meaning of his life?

[a] from *Summer's Last Will and Testament*

Song

Adieu, farewell earth's bliss,
This world uncertain is;
Fond are life's lustful joys,
Death proves them all but toys,
None from his darts can fly.
I am sick, I must die.
    Lord have mercy on us!

Rich men, trust not in wealth,
Gold cannot buy your health;
Physic himself must fade,
All things to end are made.
The plague full swift goes by;
I am sick, I must die.
    Lord have mercy on us!

Beauty is but a flower
Which wrinkles will devour:
Brightness falls from the air,
Queens have died young and fair,
Dust hath closed Helen's eye.
I am sick, I must die.
    Lord have mercy on us!

Strength stoops unto the grave,
Worms feed on Hector brave,
Swords may not fight with fate.
Earth still holds ope her gate;
Come! come! the bells do cry.
I am sick, I must die.
    Lord have mercy on us!

Wit with his wantonness
Tasteth death's bitterness;
Hell's executioner
Hath no ears for to hear
What vain art can reply.
I am sick, I must die.
    Lord have mercy on us!

Haste, therefore, each degree,
To welcome destiny.
Heaven is our heritage,
Earth but a player's stage;
Mount we unto the sky.
I am sick, I must die.
    Lord have mercy on us!

[**b**] Conjectural reading of *Song*, third stanza

Beauty is but a flower
Which wrinkles will devour:
Brightness falls from the hair,
Queens have died young and fair,
Dust hath closed Helen's eye.
I am sick, I must die.
    Lord have mercy on us!

The third stanza of Nashe's poem written in time of plague is
often anthologized separately. Yet it has been argued, by
J. V. Cunningham in *Tradition and Poetic Structure* (Swallow,
1960, p. 53), that its most famous line, 'Brightness falls from the
air'—one of the most beautiful lines in English lyric poetry—is
a corruption. His argument is that the poem is built up, line
after line, by a number of fairly literal and unfigurative pro-
positions. 'Brightness falls from the *hair*' is 'a literal account of
the effect of age and death', of the same order as 'Queens have
died young and fair' and all the other propositions. The line
as commonly printed is too romantic, too much in the symbolist

tradition, for us to accept it as correct. 'There is no doubt . . . as to the correct reading. In fact, the symbolist line, however good, is a bad line in context since it is out of keeping.'

I am afraid that his conjecture is probably correct. But I also feel that, even if it were proved up to the hilt, we should not exchange the dazzling mixture of similarity and dissimilarity created by the association of the cosmic meteor image with 'dust' and 'Helen's eye' for a commonplace image which also has an unfortunate suggestion of dandruff! Does a poet have any rights in his poem, once it is given to the world? The Eskimos, it is worth mentioning, believe that a poet owns his poem only until his death.

Part III

crossings

translations, transliterations, related poems

from *The Odyssey*, XXIV, 1-14

[a] GEORGE CHAPMAN

Cyllenian Hermes, with his golden rod,
The Wooers' souls, that yet retain'd abode
Amidst their bodies, call'd in dreadful rout
Forth to th'Infernals; who came murmuring out.
And as amidst the desolate retreat
Of some vast cavern, made the sacred seat
Of austere spirits, bats with breasts and wings
Clasp fast the walls, and each to other clings,
But, swept off from their coverts, up they rise
And fly with murmurs in amazeful guise
About the cavern; so these, grumbling, rose
And flock'd together. Down before them goes
None-hurting Mercury to Hell's broad ways,
And straight to those straits, where the ocean stays
His lofty current in calm deeps, they flew.
Then to the snowy rock they next withdrew,
And to the close of Phoebus' orient gates.
The nation then of dreams, and then the states
Of those souls' idols that the weary dead
Gave up in earth, which in a flow'ry mead
Had habitable situatión.

―――――――

[b] WILLIAM COWPER

And now Cyllenian Hermes summon'd forth
The spirits of the suitors; waving wide
The golden wand of power to seal all eyes
In slumber, and to ope them wide again,
He drove them gibbering down into the shades.
As when the bats within some hallow'd cave
Flit squeaking all around, for if but one
Fall from the rock, the rest all follow him,

In such connexion mutual they adhere;
So, after bounteous Mercury, the ghosts
Troop'd downward gibbering all the dreary way.
The Ocean's flood and the Leucadian rock,
The Sun's gate also and the land of Dreams
They pass'd, whence next into the meads they came
Of Asphodel, by shadowy forms possess'd,
Simulars of the dead.

---

[c] WILLIAM MORRIS

But now the ghosts of the men who were of the wooers' band
Called forth Cyllenian Hermes; and he had his staff in hand,
Lovely and golden, wherewith he lulleth the eyes of men,
Whomsoever he willeth, while others from slumber he
    rouseth again.
Therewith he roused and drave them, who gibbering went
    along;
As when in the inmost ingle of a wondrous den the throng
Of night-bats gibbereth fluttering, when one falleth off aloof
From their chain, where clustered together they hang from
    the rocky roof,
So fared their flock a-twittering, and Hermes void of wrong
Adown the dusky highway led all the band along:
There by the streams of Ocean and the White Rock went
    their band,
By the gates of the Sun they wended and by the dream-folk's
    land,
Till in no long while they were gotten to the meads of
    asphodel,
Wherein the ghosts, the pictures of outworn men-folk, dwell.

Meanwhile the suitors' ghosts were called away
by Hermês of Kyllênê, bearing the golden wand
with which he charms the eyes of men or wakens
whom he wills.
            He waved them on, all squeaking
as bats will in a cavern's underworld,
all flitting, flitting criss-cross in the dark
if one falls and the rock-hung chain is broken.
So with faint cries the shades trailed after Hermês,
pure Deliverer.

                He led them down dank ways,
over grey Ocean tides, the Snowy Rock,
past shores of Dream and narrows of the sunset,
in swift flight to where the Dead inhabit
wastes of asphodel at the world's end.

Meanwhile Cyllenian Hermes was gathering in the souls of the
Suitors, armed with the splendid golden wand that he can use
at will to cast a spell on our eyes or wake us from the soundest
sleep. He roused them up and marshalled them with this, and
they obeyed his summons gibbering like bats that squeak and
flutter in the depths of some mysterious cave when one of them
has fallen from the rocky roof, losing his hold on his clustered
friends. With such shrill discord the company set out in Hermes'
charge, following the Deliverer down the dark paths of decay.
Past Ocean Stream, past the White Rock, past the Gates of the
Sun and the region of dreams they went, and before long they
reached the meadow of asphodel, which is the dwelling-place of
souls, the disembodied wraiths of men.

Odysseus, reaching home after the Trojan War, has slain the Suitors who have been battening off Penelope.

As we should expect, the rhymed translations find it most difficult to convey the sense of the original. Thus, Chapman omits the description of the golden rod's power, and makes the bats far too material by giving them breasts and wings. Morris translates everything correctly, except for reversing the subject and object of the first sentence; but he also includes much that is simply William Morris, or simply padding, or both. Of all poetic elements, imagery stands the best chance of surviving the carnage of translation; and Homer's great simile of the bats survives in all these versions.

E. V. Rieu's prose translation gives a good impression of the literal sense.

[a] from *Alturas de Macchu Picchu*

Muertos de un solo abismo, sombras de una
    hondonada,
la profunda, es así como al tamaño
de vuestra magnitud
vino la verdadera, la más abrasadora
muerte y desde las rocas taladradas,
desde los capiteles escarlata,
desde los acueductos escalares
os desplomasteis como en un otoño
en una sola muerte.
Hoy el aire vacío ya no llora,
ya no conoce vuestros pies de arcilla,
ya olvidó vuestros cántaros que filtraban el cielo
cuando lo derramaban los cuchillos del rayo,
y el árbol poderoso fué comido
por la niebla, y cortado por la racha.
Él sostuvo una mano que cayó de repente
desde la altura hasta el final del tiempo.
Ya no sois, manos de araña, débiles
hebras, tela enmarañada:
cuanto fuistes cayó: costumbres, sílabas
raídas, máscaras de luz deslumbradora.

Pero una permanencia de piedra y de palabra:
la ciudad como un vaso se levantó en las manos
de todos, vivos, muertos, callados, sostenidos
de tanta muerte, un muro, de tanta vida un golpe
de pétalos de piedra: la rosa permanente, la morada:
este arrecife andino de colonias glaciales.

Cuando la mano de color de arcilla
se convirtió en arcilla, y cuando los pequeños párpados
    se cerraron
llenos de ásperos muros, poblados de castillos,
y cuando todo el hombre se enredó en su agujero,
quedó la exactitud enarbolada:
el alto sitio de la aurora humana:
la más alta vasija que contuvo el silencio:
una vida de piedra después de tantas vidas.

[**b**] Translated by BEN BELITT

from *The Heights of Macchu Picchu*

O you dead of a common abysm, shades of a chasm,
see where the depths lead! it is this way: as if
to your magnitudes's measure,
death's perfectness came in the quick of a holocaust;
as if, from the ravage
of drillers, the crimson pilasters
and staggered ascents of the aqueducts,
you veered out of plumb, indivisibly
dying, and crashed like an autumn.
The hollow of air will lament you no longer,
nor acknowledge the chalk of your footfalls;
your cruses that filtered the sky
brimming the light with a sunburst of knives,
are forgotten; the power that lives in the tree
is devoured by the haze and struck down by the wind.
Suddenly, out of the summits, into uttermost time,
the hand that it cradled has toppled.
All that spidery finger-play, the gimcrack
device of the fibres, the meshes' entanglements—you have
    put them behind.
All that you were, falls away: habitudes, tatterdemalion
syllables, the blinding personae of light.

We come upon permanence: the rock that abides and the
    word:
the city upraised like a cup in our fingers,
all hands together, the quick and the dead and the quietened;
    death's
plenitude holding us here, a bastion, the fullness
of life like a blow falling, petals of flint
and the perduring rose, abodes for the sojourner.
a glacier for multitudes, breakwater in Andes.

Now when the clay-colored hand is made
one with the clay, diminutive eyelids close over,
crammed with the bruise of the walls, peopled with castles,
as if our humanity tangled itself in a bog—
a leafy exactitude stays:
the high places, holding our human beginnings:
that steepest alembic encircling our silence:
life like an adamant, after the fleeting of lives.

———————

[c] Translated by NATHANIEL TARN

You dead of a common abyss, shades of one ravine—
the deepest—as if to match
the compass of your magnitude,
this is how it came, the true, the most consuming death:
from perforated rocks
from crimson cornices,
and cataracting aqueducts,
you plummeted like an autumn
into a single death.
Today the vacant air no longer mourns
nor knows your shard-like feet,
forgets your pitchers that filtered the sky
when the knives of the lightning ripped it open
and the powerful tree was devoured
by mist and felled by wind.
It sustained a hand that suddenly pitched
from the heights to the depths of time.
You no longer exist: spider fingers, frail

threads, tangled cloth—everything you were
dropped away: customs and tattered
syllables, the dazzling masks of light.

And yet a permanence of stone and language
upheld the city raised like a chalice
in all those hands: live, dead and stilled,
aloft with so much death, a wall, with so much life,
struck with flint petals: the everlasting rose, our home,
this reef on Andes, its glacial territories.

On the day the clay-coloured hand
was utterly changed into clay, and when dwarf eyelids closed
upon bruised walls and hosts of battlements,
when all of man in us cringed back into its burrow—
there remained a precision unfurled
on the high places of the human dawn,
the tallest crucible that ever held our silence,
a life of stone after so many lives.

———————————

Macchu Picchu is an ancient, perhaps the most ancient, city of
the Incas. Its stupendous monolithic ruins are set in the gran-
deur of the Andes. As a Peruvian, Neruda is meditating on the
great past of his race.

Spanish is a more melodic language than English. Ben Belitt's
translation strikingly imitates the rhythmic and alliterative
qualities of Neruda's poem, but in so doing runs the risk of
straining against the nature of English, and of altering the sense.
To take the last line as an example: 'Life like an ádamant, àfter
the fléeting of líves' is much closer in sound to the Spanish than
is 'A life of stone after so many lives'. But the Belitt has a
'poetical' air, a slight feeling of artifice, that the native Spanish
does not have nor want to have. Tarn's line, in contrast,
sacrifices melodic similarity, but has the equivalent *English* tone
to the Neruda—a hard economy of statement—and is more
accurate ('adamant' and 'fleeting of' are not in the original).
Such sacrifices are inevitable, and to my mind both translations
are excellent.

31 RAINER MARIA RILKE

Orpheus. Eurydice. Hermes

[a] Translated by J. B. LEISHMAN

That was the strange unfathomed mine of souls.
And they, like silent veins of silver ore,
were winding through its darkness. Between roots
welled up the blood that flows on to mankind,
like blocks of heavy porphyry in the darkness.
Else there was nothing red.

But there were rocks
and ghostly forests. Bridges over voidness
and that immense, grey, unreflecting pool
that hung above its so far distant bed
like a grey rainy sky above a landscape.
And between meadows, soft and full of patience,
appeared the pale strip of the single pathway
like a long line of linen laid to bleach.

And on this single pathway they approached.

In front the slender man in the blue mantle,
gazing in dumb impatience straight before him.
His steps devoured the way in mighty chunks
they did not pause to chew; his hands were hanging,
heavy and clenched, out of the falling folds,
no longer conscious of the lightsome lyre,
the lyre which had grown into his left
like twines of rose into a branch of olive.
It seemed as though his senses were divided:
for, while his sight ran like a dog before him,
turned round, came back, and stood, time and again,
distant and waiting, at the path's next turn,
his hearing lagged behind him like a smell.
It seemed to him at times as though it stretched
back to the progress of those other two
who should be following up this whole ascent.
Then once more there was nothing else behind him

117

but his climb's echo and his mantle's wind.
He, though, assured himself they still were coming;
said it aloud and heard it die away.
They still were coming, only they were two
that trod with fearful lightness. If he durst
but once look back (if only looking back
were not undoing of this whole enterprise
still to be done), he could not fail to see them,
the two light-footers, following him in silence:

The god of faring and of distant message,
the travelling-hood over his shining eyes,
the slender wand held out before his body,
the wings around his ankles lightly beating,
and in his left hand, as entrusted, *her*.

She, so belov'd, that from a single lyre
more mourning rose than from all women-mourners,—
that a whole world of mourning rose, wherein
all things were once more present: wood and vale
and road and hamlet, field and stream and beast,—
and that around this world of mourning turned,
even as around the other earth, a sun
and a whole silent heaven full of stars,
a heaven of mourning with disfigured stars:—
she, so beloved.

But hand in hand now with that god she walked,
her paces circumscribed by lengthy shroudings,
uncertain, gentle, and without impatience.
Wrapt in herself, like one whose time is near,
she thought not of the man who went before them,
nor of the road ascending into life.
Wrapt in herself she wandered. And her deadness
was filling her like fullness.
Full as a fruit with sweetness and with darkness
was she with her great death, which was so new
that for the time she could take nothing in.

She had attained a new virginity
and was intangible; her sex had closed
like a young flower at the approach of evening,
and her pale hands had grown so disaccustomed
to being a wife, that even the slim god's
endlessly gentle contact as he led her
disturbed her like a too great intimacy.

Even now she was no longer that blonde woman
who'd sometimes echoed in the poet's poems,
no longer the broad couch's scent and island,
nor yonder man's possession any longer.

She was already loosened like long hair,
And given far and wide like fallen rain,
and dealt out like a manifold supply.

She was already root.

And when abruptly,
the god had halted her and, with an anguished
outcry, outspoke the words: He has turned round!—
she took in nothing, and said softly: Who?

But in the distance, dark in the bright exit,
someone or other stood, whose countenance
was indistinguishable. Stood and saw
how, on a strip of pathway between meadows,
with sorrow in his look, the god of message
turned silently to go behind the figure
already going back by that same pathway,
its paces circumscribed by lengthy shroudings,
uncertain, gentle, and without impatience.

———————

That's the strange regalia of souls.
Vibrant
as platinum filaments they went,
like arteries through their darkness. From the holes
of powder beetles, from the otter's bed,
from the oak king judging by the royal oak—
blood like our own life-blood, sprang.
Otherwise nothing was red.

The dark was heavier than Caesar's foot.

There were canyons there,
distracted forests, and bridges over air-pockets;
a great gray, blind lake
moaned over the background canals,
like a bag of winds over the Caucasus.
Through terraced highlands, stocked with cattle and patience,
streaked the single road.
It was unwinding like a bandage.

They went on this road.

First the willowy man in the blue cloak;
he didn't say a thing. He counted his toes.
His step ate up the road,
a yard at a time, without bruising a thistle. His hands fell,
clammy and clenched,
as if they feared the folds of his tunic,
as if they didn't know a thing about the frail lyre,
hooked on his left shoulder,
like roses wrestling an olive tree.

It was as though his intelligence were cut in two.
His outlook worried like a dog behind him,
now diving ahead, now romping back,
now yawning on its haunches at an elbow of the road.
What he heard breathed myrrh behind him,
and often it seemed to reach back to them.
those two others

on oath to follow behind to the finish.
Then again there was nothing behind him,
only the backring of his heel,
and the currents of air in his blue cloak.
He said to himself, 'For all that, they are there.'
He spoke aloud and heard his own voice die.
'They are coming, but if they are two,
how fearfully light their step is!'
Couldn't he turn round? (Yet a single back-look
would be the ruin of this work
so near perfection.) And as a matter of fact,
he knew he must now turn to them, those two light ones,
who followed and kept their counsel.
First the road-god, the messenger man . . .
His caduceus shadow-bowing behind him,
his eye arched archaic,
his ankles feathered like arrows—
in his left hand he held *her*,
the one so loved that out of a single lyre
more sorrow came than from all women in labour,

so that out of this sorrow came
the fountain-head of the world: valleys, fields,
towns, roads . . . acropolis,
marble quarries, goats, vineyards.
And this sorrow-world circled about her,
just as the sun and stern stars
circle the earth—
a heaven of anxiety ringed by the determined stars . . .
that's how *she* was.

She leant, however, on the god's arm;
her step was delicate from her wound—
uncertain, drugged and patient.
She was drowned in herself, as in a higher hope,
and she didn't give the man in front of her a thought,
nor the road climbing to life.
She was in herself. Being dead
fulfilled her beyond fulfilment.
Like an apple full of sugar and darkness,
she was full of her decisive death,

so green she couldn't bite into it.
She was still in her marble maidenhood,
untouchable. Her sex had closed house,
like a young flower rebuking the night air.
Her hands were still ringing and tingling—
even the light touch of the god
was almost a violation.

A woman?
She was no longer that blond transcendence
so often ornamenting the singer's metres,
nor a hanging garden in his double bed.
She had wearied of being the hero's one possession.

She was as bountiful as uncoiled hair,
poured out like rain,
shared in a hundred pieces like her wedding cake.

She was a root, self-rooted.

And when the god suddenly gripped her,
and said with pain in his voice, 'He is looking back at us,'
she didn't get through to the words,
and answered vaguely, 'Who?'

Far there, dark against the clear entrance,
stood some one, or rather no one
you'd ever know. He stood and stared
at the one level, inevitable road,
as the reproachful god of messengers
looking round, pushed off again.
His caduceus was like a shotgun on his shoulder.

J. B. Leishman's is a translation as faithful to the original as he
can make it; Robert Lowell's is an 'imitation'. It is his own
term for the genre he has created: a poem which is part original
and part translation. Lowell's modernism in language and
metaphor stretches out the poem, like a man on the rack,
between the archetypal myth and contemporary reality. He has
grafted uneasy mid-century America on to Rilke's already pro-
found re-interpretation of the myth.

[a] *Song LXXXV*

> Odi et amo. quare id faciam, fortasse requiris.
> nescio, sed fieri sentio et excrucior.

---

[b] Translated by PETER WHIGHAM

> I hate and I love. And if you ask me how,
> I do not know: I only feel it, and I'm torn in two.

---

[c] Translated by CELIA and LOUIS ZUKOVSKY

O th'hate I move love. Quarry it fact I am, for that's so re
    queries.
Nescience, say th'fiery scent I owe whets crookeder.

The Zukovsky translation is an attempt to follow 'the sound,
rhythm and syntax of his Latin . . . to breathe the "literal"
meaning with his'. Peter Whigham's translation, faithful to the
sense, cannot convey all the sound qualities of the original, the
spitting alliterative 'f's and harsh 'k's, the rapid syllables; the
Zukovskys, closer to the muscular feel of the poem though much
more clotted than the Latin, have to sacrifice most of the sense.

A poem rests in its own language as naturally as a heart in its
body. It is astonishing, really, that so many transplants are not
total failures. The comparatively good success-rate, or at least
nonfailure-rate, is probably due to sound's mysterious half-
dependence on sense; 'swallow', for example, only sounds
lovely when we connect it with bird-flight and not medicine.

LDMN analysis of Thomas Nashe's *Song* (see **28** [**a**], p. 103)

```
D,  LL    L,
LD  NN   ,
ND    L  LLL  ,
D    M  LL        ,
NN  M    D  N  L,
M  ,    M  D :
        LD    M  N  .


MN,    N  N  L,
LD  NN        L,
ML  M  D .
LL  N,    ND    MD ,
L  LL        ,
M  ,    M  D :
        LD    M  N  .


L,
NL  LL  D ,
N  LL  M    ,
N    DD  N ,  ND  ,
D    LD  LN  .
M  ,    M  D :
        LD    M  N  .


N    N  ,
M  D  N    ,
D  M  N      ,
LL  LD      .
M ,  M ,    LL  D  .
M  ,    M  D :
        LD    M  N  .
```

NN,
D N :
L N,
N
N   N L.
M ,   M D:
     LD   M N .

D,
LM DN :
N   ,
L   ,
MN   N   .
M ,   M D:
     LD M N .

George MacBeth's poem should be read aloud, with careful
attention to the punctuation and spacing; e.g. 'dee, . . . ell-ell
. . . . . . ell'. Double-letters, as in 'farewell', are given double
value. Doubling of consonants is much more frequent in
Elizabethan English than in modern, and may indicate a more
forceful pronunciation; surely, though, not twice as forceful,
and to a degree this poem for the voice is paying tribute to
poetry for the eye—the appearance of a poem on the page is a
part of its meaning. But primarily the analysis explores some
elements of a famous lyric's subtle music, and the emotional
qualities of certain pure sounds.

Nashe's *Song* has been analysed in its original Elizabethan
orthography, which accounts for a few apparent inconsistencies.

from *Antonius*, translated by Thomas North

Therefore when she was sent unto by divers letters, both from
Antonius himself, and also from his friends, she made so light
of it and mocked Antonius so much, that she disdained to set
forward otherwise, but to take her barge in the river of Cydnus,
the poop whereof was of gold, the sails of purple, and the oars of
silver, which kept stroke in rowing after the sounds of the music
of flutes, hautboys, citherns, viols, and such other instruments
as they played upon in the barge. And now for the person of her
self: she was laid under a pavilion of cloth of gold of tissue,
apparelled and attired like the goddess Venus, commonly
drawn in picture: and hard by her, on either hand of her,
pretty fair boys apparelled as painters do set forth god Cupid,
with little fans in their hands, with the which they fanned wind
upon her. Her ladies and gentlewomen also, the fairest of them
were apparelled like the nymphs Nereides (which are the mer-
maids of the waters) and like the Graces, some steering the
helm, others tending the tackle and ropes of the barge, out of
the which there came a wonderful passing sweet savour of
perfumes, that perfumed the wharf's side, pestered with in-
numerable multitudes of people. Some of them followed the
barge all along the river's side: others also ran out of the city
to see her coming in. So that in the end, there ran such multi-
tudes of people one after another to see her, that Antonius was
left post alone in the market place, in his Imperial seat to give
audience: and there went a rumour in the people's mouths,
that the goddess Venus was come to play with the god Bacchus,
for the general good of all Asia.

from *Antony and Cleopatra*, II.ii.194–223

ENOBARBUS: I will tell you.
    The barge she sat in, like a burnish'd throne,
    Burnt on the water: the poop was beaten gold;
    Purple the sails, and so perfumed that
    The winds were love-sick with them; the oars were silver,
    Which to the tune of flutes kept stroke, and made
    The water which they beat to follow faster,
    As amorous of their strokes. For her own person,
    It beggar'd all description: she did lie
    In her pavilion—cloth-of-gold of tissue—
    O'er-picturing that Venus where we see
    The fancy outwork nature: on each side her
    Stood pretty dimpled boys, like smiling Cupids,
    With divers-colour'd fans, whose wind did seem
    To glow the delicate cheeks which they did cool,
    And what they undid did.
AGRIPPA: O, rare for Anthony!

ENOBARBUS: Her gentlewomen, like the Nereides,
    So many mermaids, tended her i' the eyes,
    And made their bends adornings: at the helm
    A seeming mermaid steers: the silken tackle
    Swell with the touches of those flower-soft hands
    That yarely frame the office. From the barge
    A strange invisible perfume hits the sense
    Of the adjacent wharfs. The city cast
    Her people out upon her; and Anthony,
    Enthron'd i'the market-place, did sit alone,
    Whistling to the air; which, but for vacancy,
    Had gone to gaze on Cleopatra too,
    And made a gap in nature.

from *All for Love*, III.i.164–184

ANTONY: Her galley down the silver Cydnus rowed,
    The tackling silk, the streamers waved with gold;
    The gentle winds were lodged in purple sails:
    Her nymphs, like Nereids, round her couch were placed;
    Where she, another sea-born Venus, lay.
DOLABELLA: No more; I would not hear it.
ANTONY: Oh, you must!
    She lay, and leant her cheek upon her hand,
    And cast a look so languishingly sweet,
    As if, secure of all beholders' hearts,
    Neglecting, she could take them: boys, like Cupids,
    Stood fanning, with their painted wings, the winds,
    That played about her face. But if she smiled,
    A darting glory seemed to blaze abroad,
    That men's desiring eyes were never wearied,
    But hung upon the object: To soft flutes
    The silver oars kept time; and while they played,
    The hearing gave new pleasure to the sight;
    And both to thought. 'Twas heaven, or somewhat more:
    For she so charmed all hearts, that gazing crowds
    Stood panting on the shore, and wanted breath
    To give their welcome voice.

One Cydnus, but three Cleopatras. Plutarch's is the Cleopatra of history, or historical fiction; Shakespeare has invented nothing and transfigured everything; Dryden's Cleopatra is a languid, charming Restoration lady. If we look, for example, at the three accounts of the boys fanning her, the described action is the same, yet the feeling in each, and the impact it has on us, is totally different. Shakespeare's verse seems to move through language and experience in the manner of a plane's reconaissance as against a car's; a difference in kind rather than degree from the verse of other, even major, poets. Theirs moves along already laid roads of grammar and convention; his makes its own flightpath, and great swathes of country open out all round its shadow.

[a] from *Romeo and Juliet*, III.v.1–36

JULIET: Wilt thou be gone? it is not yet near day:
It was the nightingale, and not the lark,
That pierc'd the fearful hollow of thine ear;
Nightly she sings on yond pomegranate-tree:
Believe me, love, it was the nightingale.
ROMEO: It was the lark, the herald of the morn,
No nightingale: look, love, what envious streaks
Do lace the severing clouds in yonder east:
Night's candles are burnt out, and jocund day
Stands tiptoe on the misty mountain tops.
I must be gone and live, or stay and die.
JULIET: Yond light is not day-light, I know it, I:
It is some meteor that the sun exhales,
To be to thee this night a torch-bearer,
And light thee on thy way to Mantua:
Therefore stay yet,—thou need'st not to be gone.
ROMEO: Let me be ta'en, let me be put to death;
I am content, so thou wilt have it so.
I'll say yon gray is not the morning's eye,
'Tis but the pale reflex of Cynthia's brow;
Nor that is not the lark, whose notes do beat
The vaulty heaven so high above our heads:
I have more care to stay than will to go:—
Come, death, and welcome! Juliet wills it so.—
How is't, my soul? let's talk,—it is not day.
JULIET: It is, it is,—hie hence, be gone, away!
It is the lark that sings so out of tune,
Straining harsh discords and unpleasing sharps.
Some say the lark makes sweet division;
This doth not so, for she divideth us:
Some say the lark and loathed toad change eyes;
O, now I would they had chang'd voices too!
Since arm from arm that voice doth us affray,
Hunting thee hence with hunt's-up to the day.
O, now be gone; more light and light it grows.
ROMEO: More light and light,—more dark and dark our woes!

Parting

HE: Dear, I must be gone
While night shuts the eyes
Of the household spies;
That song announces dawn.

SHE: No, night's bird and love's
Bids all true lovers rest,
While his loud song reproves
The murderous stealth of day.

HE: Daylight already flies
From mountain crest to crest.

SHE: That light is from the moon.

HE: That bird . . .

SHE: Let him sing on,
I offer to love's play
My dark declivities.

― ― ―

Parting is obviously based very closely on the scene from *Romeo and Juliet*. Since not even Yeats could equal the lyrical beauty of the original, what has he achieved by isolating part of the counterpointed emotions? What is so strange, and strangely affecting, about the concluding line?

[a] from *Pericles*, V.i.62–235

Enter, from the barge, FIRST LORD, with MARINA and a young
LADY.

LYSIMACHUS: O, here is
 The lady that I sent for.—Welcome, fair one!—
 Is't not a goodly presence?
HELICANUS: She's a gallant lady.
LYSIMACHUS: She's such a one, that, were I well assured
 Came of a gentle kind and noble stock,
 I'ld wish no better choice, and think me rarely wed.—
 Fair one, all goodness that consists in bounty
 Expect even here, where is a kingly patient:
 If that thy prosperous and artificial feat
 Can draw him but to answer thee in aught,
 Thy sacred physic shall receive such pay
 As thy desires can wish.
MARINA: Sir, I will use
 My utmost skill in his recovery,
 Provided
 That none but I and my companion maid
 Be suffer'd to come near him.
LYSIMACHUS: Come, let's leave her;
 And the gods make her prosperous!
                                        (Marina sings.)
LYSIMACHUS: Mark'd he your music?
MARINA: No, nor look'd on us.
LYSIMACHUS: See, she will speak to him.
MARINA: Hail, sir! my lord, lend ear.
PERICLES: Hum, ha!
MARINA: I am a maid,
 My lord, that ne'er before invited eyes,
 But have been gaz'd on like a comet: she speaks,
 My lord, that, may be, hath endured a grief
 Might equal yours, if both were justly weigh'd.
 Though wayward fortune did malign my state,
 My derivation was from ancestors

131

Who stood equivalent with mighty kings:
But time hath rooted out my parentage,
And to the world and awkward casualties
Bound me in servitude.—(*aside*) I will desist;
But there is something glows upon my cheek,
And whispers in mine ear, 'Go not till he speak.'
PERICLES: My fortunes—parentage—good parentage—
To equal mine!—was it not thus? what say you?
MARINA: I said, my lord, if you did know my parentage,
You would not do me violence.
PERICLES: I do think so.—Pray you, turn your eyes upon me.
You are like something that—What countrywoman?
Here of these shores?
MARINA: No, nor of any shores:
Yet I was mortally brought forth, and am
No other than I appear.
PERICLES: I am great with woe, and shall deliver weeping.
My dearest wife was like this maid, and such a one
My daughter might have been: my queen's square
        brows;
Her stature to an inch; as wand-like straight;
As silver-voic'd; her eyes as jewel-like,
And cas'd as richly; in pace another Juno;
Who starves the ears she feeds, and makes them hungry,
The more she gives them speech.—Where do you live?
MARINA: Where I am but a stranger: from the deck
You may discern the place.
PERICLES: Where were you bred?
And how achiev'd you these endowments, which
You make more rich to owe?
MARINA: If I should tell my history, it would seem
Like lies disdain'd in the reporting.
PERICLES: Prithee, speak:
Falseness cannot come from thee; for thou look'st
Modest as Justice, and thou seem'st a palace
For the crown'd Truth to dwell in: I will believe thee,
And make my senses credit thy relation
To points that seem impossible; for thou look'st
Like one I lov'd indeed. What were thy friends?
Didst thou not say, when I did push thee back,—

Which was when I perceiv'd thee,—that thou camest
From good descending?
MARINA: So indeed I did.
PERICLES: Report thy parentage. I think thou said'st
    Thou hadst been toss'd from wrong to injury,
    And that thou thought'st thy griefs might equal
        mine,
    If both were open'd.
MARINA: Some such thing
    I said, and said no more but what my thoughts
    Did warrant me was likely.
PERICLES: Tell thy story;
    If thine consider'd prove the thousandth part
    Of my endurance, thou art a man, and I
    Have suffer'd like a girl: yet thou dost look
    Like Patience gazing on kings' graves, and smiling
    Extremity out of act. What were thy friends?
    How lost thou them? Thy name, my most kind virgin?
    Recount, I do beseech thee: come, sit by me.
MARINA: My name is Marina.
PERICLES: O, I am mock'd,
    And thou by some incensed god sent hither
    To make the world to laugh at me.
MARINA: Patience, good sir,
    Or here I'll cease.
PERICLES: Nay, I'll be patient.
    Thou little know'st how thou dost startle me,
    To call thyself Marina.
MARINA: The name
    Was given me by one that had some power,—
    My father, and a king.
PERICLES: How! a king's daughter?
    And call'd Marina?
MARINA: You said you would believe me,
    But, not to be a troubler of your peace,
    I will end here.
PERICLES: But are you flesh and blood?
    Have you a working pulse? and are no fairy?
    Motion!—well; speak on. Where were you born?
    And wherefore call'd Marina?

133

MARINA: Call'd Marina
    For I was born at sea.
PERICLES: At sea! what mother?
MARINA: My mother was the daughter of a king;
    Who died the minute I was born,
    As my good nurse Lychorida hath oft
    Deliver'd weeping.
PERICLES: O, stop there a little!—
    (*aside*) This is the rarest dream that e'er dull sleep
    Did mock sad fools withal: this cannot be:
    My daughter's buried.—Well:—where were you bred?
    I'll hear you more, to the bottom of your story,
    And never interrupt you.
MARINA: You scorn: believe me, 'twere best I did give o'er.
PERICLES: I will believe you by the syllable
    Of what you shall deliver. Yet, give me leave:—
    How came you in these parts? where were you bred?
MARINA: The king my father did in Tarsus leave me;
    Till cruel Cleon, with his wicked wife,
    Did seek to murder me: and having woo'd
    A villain to attempt it, who having drawn to do't,
    A crew of pirates came and rescued me;
    Brought me to Mytilene. But, good sir,
    Whither will you have me? Why do you weep? It may be
    You think me an imposter: no, good faith,
    I am the daughter to King Pericles,
    If good King Pericles be.
PERICLES: Ho, Helicanus!
HELICANUS: Calls my lord?
PERICLES: Thou art a grave and noble counsellor,
    Most wise in general: tell me, if thou canst,
    What this maid is, or what is like to be,
    That thus hath made me weep?
HELICANUS: I know not; but
    Here is the regent, sir, of Mytilene
    Speaks nobly of her.
LYSIMACHUS: She never would tell
    Her parentage; being demanded that,
    She would sit still and weep.
PERICLES: O Helicanus, strike me, honour'd sir;

Give me a gash, put me to present pain;
Lest this great sea of joys rushing upon me
O'erbear the shores of my mortality,
And drown me with their sweetness.—O, come
  hither,
Thou that begett'st him that did thee beget;
Thou that wast born at sea, buried at Tarsus,
And found at sea again!—O Helicanus,
Down on thy knees, thank the holy gods as loud
As thunder threatens us: this is Marina.—
What was thy mother's name? tell me but that,
For truth can never be confirm'd enough,
Though doubts did ever sleep.

MARINA: First, sir, I pray,
What is your title?

PERICLES: I am Pericles of Tyre: but tell me now
My drown'd queen's name, as in the rest you said
Thou hast been godlike perfect:
Be heir of kingdoms, and another life
To Pericles thy father.

MARINA: Is it no more to be your daughter than
To say my mother's name was Thaisa?
Thaisa was my mother, who did end
The minute I began.

PERICLES: Now, blessing on thee! rise; thou art my child.—
Give me fresh garments.—Mine own, Helicanus,—
She is not dead at Tarsus, as she would have been,
By savage Cleon: she shall tell thee all;
When thou shalt kneel, and justify in knowledge
She is thy very princess.—Who is this?

HELICANUS: Sir, 'tis the governor of Mytilene,
Who, hearing of your melancholy state,
Did come to see you.

PERICLES: I embrace you.
Give me my robes.—I am wild in my beholding.—
O heavens bless my girl!—But, hark, what music?—
Tell Helicanus, my Marina, tell him
O'er, point by point, for yet he seems to doubt,
How sure you are my daughter.—But, what music?

HELICANUS: My lord, I hear none.

PERICLES: None!

    The music of the spheres!—List, my Marina.

LYSIMACHUS: It is not good to cross him; give him way.

PERICLES: Rarest sounds! Do ye not hear?

LYSIMACHUS: My lord, I hear.

                                              (Music.)

PERICLES: Most heavenly music!

    It nips me unto listening, and thick slumber

    Hangs upon mine eyes: let me rest.   (Sleeps.)

[**b**] T. S. ELIOT

Marina

Quis hic locus, quae
regio, quae mundi plaga?

What seas what shores what grey rocks and what islands
What water lapping the bow
And scent of pine and the woodthrush winging through the
    fog
What images return
O my daughter.

    Those who sharpen the tooth of the dog, meaning
Death
Those who glitter with the glory of the hummingbird,
    meaning
Death
Those who sit in the eye of contentment, meaning
Death
Those who suffer the ecstasy of the animals, meaning
Death

    Are become unsubstantial, reduced by a wind,
A breath of pine, and the woodsong fog
By this grace dissolved in place

What is this face, less clear and clearer
The pulse in the arm, less strong and stronger—
Given or lent? more distant than stars and nearer than the
    eye
Whispers and small laughter between leaves and hurrying
    feet
Under sleep, where all the waters meet.
Bowsprit cracked with ice and paint cracked with heat.
I made this, I have forgotten
And remember.
The rigging weak and the canvas rotten
Between one June and another September.
Made this unknowing, half conscious, unknown, my own.
The garboard strake leaks, the seams need caulking.
This form, this face, this life
Living to live in a world of time beyond me; let me
Resign my life for this life, my speech for that unspoken,
The awakened, lips parted, the hope, the new ships.

What seas what shores what granite islands towards my
    timbers
And woodthrush calling through the fog
My daughter.

Death and birth, suffering and joy, embrace in the final plays of
Shakespeare. The sea is both destroyer and renewer; Marina
means 'of the sea'. The storm which brought tragedy at
Marina's birth is a metaphor for the nature of life: death is
present at the moment of birth. But the converse is also true;
and life outweighs death. The death/birth cycle is expressed in
the music of the verse, which is both grave and mysteriously
joyful . . . 'I am great with woe and shall deliver weeping', a
line which Marina later echoes. The pun on 'deliver' reminds
us that Shakespeare did not always throw away a world for the
sake of a pun, as Dr Johnson accused him of doing.
    Pericles's joy at finding his daughter alive is not the false joy
of possessing; when he says, 'Mine own, Helicanus', he is not
speaking as of an object, but of a new life that his and his wife's

flesh had 'yielded'—another compressed metaphor, meaning both 'given birth to' and 'given up'.

The same joyous ambivalence—restored possession and at the same time resignation—are present in Eliot's *Marina*. The symbolism is the same in both, though Eliot's images are reminiscent of his native shore, New England. The woodthrush's call replaces Pericles's 'music of the spheres'. If any simple statement could come close to expressing the meaning of the scene and the poem, it might be these lines from Kahlil Gibran's *The Prophet*: 'Your children are not your children. / They are the sons and daughters of Life's longing for itself. / They come through you but not from you.'

The Idea of Entropy at Maenporth Beach

'C'est elle! Noire et pourtant lumineuse'

A boggy wood as full of springs as trees.
Slowly she slipped into the muck.
It was a white dress, she said, and that was not right.
Leathery polished mud, that stank as it split.
It is a smooth white body, she said, and that is not right,
Not quite right; I'll have a smoother,
Slicker body, and my golden hair
Will sprinkle rich goodness everywhere.
So slowly she backed into the mud.

If it were a white dress, she said, with some little black,
Dressed with a little flaw, a smut, some swart
Twinge of ancestry, or if it were all black
Since I am white, but—it's my mistake.
So slowly she slunk, all pleated, into the muck.

The mud spatters with rich seed and ranging pollens.
Black darts up the pleats, black pleats
Lance along the white ones, and she stops
Swaying, cut in half. Is it right, she sobs
As the fat, juicy, incredibly tart muck rises
Round her throat and dims the diamond there?
It is right, so she stretches her white neck back
And takes a deep breath once and a one step back.
Some golden strands afloat pull after her.

The mud recoils, lies heavy, queasy, swart.
But then this soft blubber stirs, and quickly she comes up
Dressed like a mound of lickerish earth,
Swiftly ascending in a streaming pat
That grows tall, smooths brimming hips, and steps out
On flowing pillars, darkly draped.
And then the blackness breaks open with blue eyes
Of this black Venus rising helmeted in night
Who as she glides grins brilliantly, and drops
Swatches superb as molasses on her path.

Who is that negress running on the beach
Laughing excitedly with teeth as white
As the white waves kneeling, dazzled, to the sands?
Clapping excitedly the black rooks rise,
Running delightedly in slapping rags
She sprinkles substance, and the small life flies!

She laughs aloud, and bares her teeth again, and cries:
Now that I am all black, and running in my richness
And knowing it a little, I have learnt
It is quite wrong to be all white always;
And knowing it a little, I shall take great care
To keep a little black about me somewhere.
A snotty nostril, a mourning nail will do.
Mud is a good dress, but not the best.
Ah, watch, she runs into the sea. She walks
In streaky white on dazzling sands that stretch
Like the whole world's pursy mud quite purged.
The black rooks coo like doves, new suns beam
From every droplet of the shattering waves,
From every crystal of the shattered rock.
Drenched in the mud, pure white rejoiced,
From this collision were new colours born,
And in their slithering passage to the sea
The shrugged-up riches of deep darkness sang.

---

[b] WALLACE STEVENS

The Idea of Order at Key West

She sang beyond the genius of the sea.
The water never formed to mind or voice,
Like a body wholly body, fluttering
Its empty sleeves; and yet its mimic motion
Made constant cry, caused constantly a cry,
That was not ours although we understood,
Inhuman, of the veritable ocean.

The sea was not a mask. No more was she.
The song and water were not medleyed sound
Even if what she sang was what she heard,
Since what she sang was uttered word by word.
It may be that in all her phrases stirred
The grinding water and the gasping wind;
But it was she and not the sea we heard.

For she was the maker of the song she sang.
The ever-hooded, tragic-gestured sea
Was merely a place by which she walked to sing.
Whose spirit is this? we said, because we knew
It was the spirit that we sought and knew
That we should ask this often as she sang.

If it was only the dark voice of the sea
That rose, or even colored by many waves;
If it was only the outer voice of sky
And cloud, of the sunken coral water-walled,
However clear, it would have been deep air,
The heaving speech of air, a summer sound
Repeated in a summer without end
And sound alone. But it was more than that,
More even than her voice, and ours, among
The meaningless plungings of water and the wind,
Theatrical distances, bronze shadows heaped
On high horizons, mountainous atmospheres
Of sky and sea.
                        It was her voice that made
The sky acutest at its vanishing.
She measured to the hour its solitude.
She was the single artificer of the world
In which she sang. And when she sang, the sea,
Whatever self it had, became the self
That was her song, for she was the maker. Then we,
As we beheld her striding there alone,
Knew that there never was a world for her
Except the one she sang and, singing, made.

Ramon Fernandez, tell me, if you know,
Why, when the singing ended and we turned
Toward the town, tell why the glassy lights,
The lights in the fishing boats at anchor there,
As the night descended, tilting in the air,
Mastered the night and portioned out the sea,
Fixing emblazoned zones and fiery poles,
Arranging, deepening, enchanting night.

Oh! Blessed rage for order, pale Ramon,
The maker's rage to order words of the sea,
Words of the fragrant portals, dimly-starred,
And of ourselves and of our origins,
In ghostlier demarcations, keener sounds.

Redgrove's title closely echoes Stevens's. Entropy is the trans-
formation of energy, the universal tendency towards disorder.
Thus the two poems are in counterpoint. The woman at
Maenporth (a beach near Falmouth, Cornwall) is grateful for
losing her pure white supremacy, slipping into the muck; she
will keep some black about her in future, even if it is only a dirty
nail. Both poems are rhapsodic. There are resemblances in style,
but also vast differences; though Redgrove's poem takes its
starting-point in Stevens's poem, it is equally original. (See
also **65**, p. 229).

from *Hamlet*, IV.vii. 65–82

There is a willow grows aslant a brook,
That shows his hoar leaves in the glassy stream;
There with fantastic garlands did she come
Of crow-flowers, nettles, daisies, and long purples
That liberal shepherds give a grosser name,
But our cold maids do dead men's fingers call them;
There, on the pendent boughs her coronet weeds
Clambering to hang, an envious sliver broke;
When down her weedy trophies and herself
Fell in the weeping brook. Her clothes spread wide,
And, mermaid-like, awhile they bore her up;
Which time she chanted snatches of old tunes,
As one incapable of her own distress,
Or like a creature native and indued
Unto that element: but long it could not be
Till that her garments, heavy with their drink,
Pull'd the poor wretch from her melodious lay
To muddy death.

---

[b] PETER REDGROVE

Young Women with the Hair of Witches and No Modesty

'I loved Ophelia!'

I have always loved water, and praised it.
I have often wished water would hold still.
Changes and glints bemuse a man terribly:
There is champagne and glimmer of mists;
Torrents, the distaffs of themselves, exalted, confused;
And snow splintering silently, skilfully, indifferently,
I have often wished water would hold still.
Now it does so, or ripples so, skilfully
In cross and doublecross, surcross and countercross.
A person lives in the darkness of it, watching gravely;

I used to see her straight and cool, considering the pond,
And as I approached she would turn gracefully
In her hair, its waves betraying her origin.
I told her that her thoughts issued in hair like consideration
    of water,
And if she laughed, that they would rain like spasms of
    weeping,
Or if she wept, then solemnly they held still,
And in the rain, the perfumes of it, and the blowing of it,
Confused, like hosts of people all shouting.
In such a world the bride walks through dressed as a
    waterfall,
And ripe grapes fall and splash smooth snow with jagged
    purple,
Young girls grow brown as acorns in their rainy climb
    towards oakhood,
And brown moths settle low down among ivories wet with
    love.
But she loosened her hair in a sudden tangle of contradictions,
In cross and doublecross, surcross and countercross,
And I was a shadow in the twilight of her late displeasure.
I asked water to stand still, now nothing else holds.

Hamlet's cry of distress and recognition—in the same instant,
it seems, realizing his love and realizing he has lost it—together
with the Queen's account of Ophelia's death by drowning,
provide the metaphor through which Peter Redgrove explores
the nature of woman and of his own attitude to her. 'Or like a
creature native and indued / Unto that element': since water
is the primeval womb of life, it *is* her element. Redgrove is
exploring Ophelia / woman / water *before* the critical change,
death, or her death to him; and his rhythm, imagery and sound
patterns express this different intention. The relationship
between the two is so subtle that if it were not for the quotation
under the title we should probably be unaware of it. The only
significant word common to both is 'weeping'. Phrases echo
each other at a distance: 'her clothes spread wide' / 'dressed as
a waterfall'; 'our cold maids' / 'I used to see her straight and

cool'; 'fell in the weeping brook' / 'ripe grapes fall'; 'but long it could not be' / 'a sudden tangle of contradictions': as distantly as the space between Shakespeare's lines and the real woman, Katherine Hamlet, whose drowning in the Avon, when Shakespeare was young, unconsciously helped to create this scene.

Sonnet

La piaga, ch'io credea che fosse salda
per la omai molta assenzia e poco amore
di quell'alpestro ed indurato core,
freddo più che di neve fredda falda,
si desta ad or ad ora e si riscalda,
e gitta ad or ad or sangue ed umore;
sì che l'alma si vive anco in timore,
ch'esser devrebbe omai sicura e balda.

Nè, perchè cerchi aggiunger novi lacci
al collo mio, so far che molto o poco
quell'antico mio nodo non m'impacci.
Si suol pur dir che foco scaccia foco;
ma tu, Amor, che'l mio martir procacci,
fai che questo in me, lassa, or non ha loco.

[The wound, which I believed to be healed by the now continued absence and slight love of that flinty, hardened heart, colder than cold sheet of snow, wakes from time to time, and grows warm, and spurts, from time to time, with blood and moistness; so that my soul still lives in fear, when it should now be safe and confident.

Nor can I in any way put new bonds to my neck, without that early knot's hindering me more or less. They often say that fire drives away fire; but you, Love, who seek my martyrdom, prevent this happening in me, weary though I be.]

Note. Gaspara Stampa (1523–54) wrote her most intense love sonnets after being rejected by her lover, a person of higher rank, and shortly before her death.

Marriage of Venice to the Sea on Ascension Day

1

Gaspara Stampa on the Bridge of Sighs.
No feeling surfaces to her cold form
That she is tortured by this meeting-place.
A hand, bloodied by nails, has drawn across

Light a rich scumble of unclearable cloud,
A golden excrement. Her god had come,
Walked on her waters; rises, vanishes.
His gold ring plunges through immensities

Into the canal whose hymen breaks.
She is left by what she is left with: love.
The artist breaks and re-sets; breaks and re-sets,
Shivering like a chain of gondolas;

From his corruption new perfections rising
To her, as a trained eye finds out new stars.

2

Till choice and chosen are suggested there,
The artist breaks, re-sets, breaks and re-sets
Her arm bent on the linen, troubling his sleep.
In excremental gold the god has come.

Now it is finished save the masterstrokes.
His gold ring plunges through immensities;
With his fingers only he perfects
The hand between her thighs, and draws across

Her upturned gaze the limits of creation.
The hymen is broken and the waters break,
The god-child breasts the breakers. He cleans his hands,

And his trained eye already finds new stars.
He turns the imperfect canvas to the wall,
Where she will find, in darkness now, his love.

147

3

The Bridge of Teats receives the water-Christ's
Benediction. Greeting the holy form,
In the film of sweat that glistens on her breasts
Each whore has traced with scarlet nail a cross.

Jesus the sun amidst white neophytes.
In golden vesture their God has come,
His gaze fixed high above San Marco's lion
As a god's vision might find out new stars.

The crowds fall to their knees. San Marco booms.
He walks the waters, rises, vanishes.
They jostle, embrace. They have seen the groom's
Gold ring flying through immensities.

The Doge puts out to sea. Gold fetors rising
Light a rich scumble of reflective cloud.

4

The lion interrupts with wilder, blue
Light the rich scumble of reflective cloud.
It is high afternoon of the young summer.
Stone walks the waters, water springs from stone.

All delight seems streaming into the city,
To celebrate a tremulous meeting-place.
Action and passion, energy and peace;
Ancient fountains free a hardening form.

Into a glazed lagoon a whore has pissed
A golden excrement. No god has come
With greater ecstasy than her affected

Shivers. Lying back in the gondola,
She takes by chance the image of Danaë,
Warm flesh-tones leaning on a bridge of sighs.

5

They rest, on the Adriatic's bluest skin,
To celebrate a tremulous meeting-place.
The cardinal prays that marriage make them dearer
As a trained eye finds out new stars.

Trumpets. The Doge opens the silver casket.
The hymen is broken and the water breaks.
Under the resettled iconostasis
A gold ring plunges through immensities.

The Doge is moved. He is that mirage
Which walks the waters, rises, vanishes.
Flambeaux flame on the galleys, augment with hymen-
Light the burnt scumble of reflective cloud

Which in the choppier waters, as dusk settles,
An artist breaks, re-sets; breaks, re-sets.

6

He must, must break his custom. Turns to him
The smiling nude. Draws a sharp breath; and sighs:
Seeing the universe concentrated where
A warm canal, beneath the illusioned form,

Secretes the shower her servant cannot catch,
And comes, with ripples like a gondola's.
Yet he, the maker's maker, cannot lie
To consummate a tremulous meeting-place,

Until reality and shadows mix
And into paint his blood is drawn across.
His old hand trembles, touches her shadowy hollow

From whose miasma new perfections rise,
As though his finger could slide in with god.
His gold ring plunges through immensities.

7

The Doge is crying. He has seen his death
Touching his life, a lovers' meeting-place,
In Titian's portrait. He smiled and gave the gold,
But shuddered. Now the chain of gondolas

Turns from the Grand Canal into his death.
The hymen is broken and the waters break.
His gondolier negotiates a canal
Unexpected, tight, like the cleft cut by love

In time's unyielding stone embattlements.
From its miasma new perfections rise
Solacing his heart. A phantom leans.
Her hand, dyked by its blood, is drawing a cross

Over her heart's decision of solitude,
As a trained eye finds out new stars.

8

A high wind blows in salt to her cloaked face.
Night's hymen's broken, her reflection breaks
Under her. A cannon's boom. Carnival shouts.
The rising flood becomes the meeting-place

Of fireflies and contagion. From her despair,
A phrase. Out of it new perfections rise.
A sonnet begins to live. From the wide sea,
Images, like the Doge's gondolas,

Negotiate into lagoons, canals.
The whole world's waters move through a cold form.
Most flows away again. Poetry's stone

Walks on the waters, rises, vanishes.
Even the flowing out she gathers in,
Building out of all loss a Venice, love.

An account of how this poem came to be written may show how various experiences can radiate towards a centre (the poem itself) like highways into a city. The radiant lines, in this case, were as follows: seeing Venice, for three hours—ample enough time to start poetry, since you experience the emotional impact without the pedantry of knowing it well; reading, later, some of Gaspara Stampa's sonnets, which moved me both in themselves and because they agitated certain personal preoccupations; and, as I started the poem, memories of Titian's painting, *Danaë and the Golden Shower*. [The painting is reproduced on the dust-jacket.] I had never before given Titian's study of creation more than a cursory glance; I think my mind recurred to it because of the nature of the ideas that were gathering round my poem—ideas of centripetal, unifying forces creating Venice at its high summer of the Renaissance, artistic creation, submission to destiny and suffering. These conceptions, together with the example of Gaspara's sonnets (one of which concludes, 'He in whom I find new perfections, / As a trained eye finds out new stars') and the feeling of ritual that I wanted to communicate, evolved a stylized form: eight sonnets linked by variant repetitions. The risk of such a form, and perhaps I have not avoided it, is that unity may be achieved at the expense of its becoming static.

The poem was nearly finished before I bothered to check whether it could have been literally possible for Gaspara to have written her sonnets of farewell to earthly love at the same time as Titian was painting Danaë. I found that, by one of those strange coincidences that happen when poems are being written —and which seem almost like an equivalent in *life* to the unify-ing processes which are going on in the art—the painting dates from 1553 and so must have been contemporaneous with the sonnets. The odds were enormously against this, and it would not have mattered poetically; all the same, I found it very moving to think that it could *actually* have happened as I had imagined it.

40 POEMS FROM A WRITING CLASS (Whitecross Comprehensive School, Hereford)

[a] Starting-point

When some stars reach an advanced age, they expand until they are Red Giants. Then they contract rapidly, implode, getting smaller and smaller until they are the size of the earth. White Dwarfs they are then called, and some stay at this size. But others go on shrinking, until they become neutron stars, only ten miles in diameter. Perhaps they stop there; but if they go on collapsing, they become Black Holes. Black Holes are like another universe, without time or space. The force of gravity is so intense that nothing sucked into one can ever escape—not even light itself. If you approached it in a space-ship, you might see other space-ships hovering on its edge—but they would not be real, only mirages. They would be the images of past space-ships sucked in, images that hang on the 'event-horizon' forever. If the Black Hole you're drawn into is stationary, you will be rapidly crushed to death; but if it is spinning, it is possible that you will survive. But you can never escape. You may go further in and through, into another universe . . . in which there will also be a Black Hole; and if you go through that, you will enter another universe, with another Black Hole. In a Black Hole nothing is as we know it. If you could move back against the spin, you would be moving back in time: you might see yourself coming in. Imagine that you are in a Black Hole. Write about how you feel.

---

[b] ROBERT LEIGHTON

The Black Hole

Where time stands still for ever.
Where prison bars are gravity.
A graveyard of Life hungry for victims,
Where death can never enter,
And Life cannot escape.

Where time stands still forever,
Where the prison has no keeper.
A graveyard of Life hungry for victims,
Where death can never enter,
And Life cannot escape.

Hopelessly forgotten in a dark eternity,
Where time taps itself on the shoulder,
Recording everything that ever was,
In the bottomless hole of nothingness.

Sound never has a meaning,
And Light is just a toy,
Where everything is nothing,
In this deep, dark, hole.

[c] NICHOLAS DAWE

The Black Hole   *Seconds of Hell*

It was not how described
not how I imagined
It was like nothing
on or off the earth
The sheer power
overwhelmed
crushed
distorted and mangled
the air was thick
crystallized like, like
walking in liquid lead
The fireless inferno
drew us ever onward
towards towards
our doom.
The sound like the
cry of a whole world in peril of destruction,
like the second after the first A bomb,
roaring
perpetual Hell.

Not long
not long to go
a few
a few seconds separated us
and that
a few seconds of eternity
doom everlasting
a crushing terrible end
like no man should die.
We'd had the universe at our finger tips
but now at death's door
all hope was lost
OH the eternal seconds
as the end loomed large
The once 15 metres thick bulkheads
subsided heralding
                    THE END or the beginning.

[d] SHAYNE POWELL

The Black Hole

The place where there is no time.
   Spinning like a top indefinitely
      No future   no past no present
         Just nothing like nothing ever
            The same things all over again
               Like a nightmare which never goes
                  Again and Again and Again
                     Unless   just say unless
   You can struggle back backwards
               Against this Joint time whirlpool
And perhaps meet your self coming forward
      Over   and over   and over again
         Like a night mare   which never goes
            Again and Again and Again.

The Black Hole

A mysterious mass of gravity
A shapeless, lightless void of energy
Eating away other planets
Killing other civilizations so it may carry on
    existing.
Inside the black hole pictures
Yes pictures just hanging in space
Images of other crafts
Like a picture museum of nothing.

Spinning constantly spinning
Nothing going round and round
But there must be something here
Nothing can't hold you captive
Entice you deeper into its black belly of death
But it is
There must be something here
Some large insane beast
Controlling the gravity pulled
Or some gigantic thing
But I see nothing so there is nothing

Deeper and Deeper I go
Falling over millions and millions of cliff tops
One small step is a gigantic leap
Down Down Down I go
Through one hole to another
And then slowly I stop
I am suspended in space for a second
I look back and see millions of me
At different stages of my fall.
And then nothing
This time there is nothing
No gravity no beasts just nothing

In giving the class (a non-Grammar stream) this starting-point for poems, I knew we would be exploring that area in which universal myth and private emotions overlap like a kind of cease-fire zone in war. For the truth about Black Holes—as astronomers dimly conceive it and as refracted and no doubt distorted through my unscientific mind—*is* myth, moving us and disturbing us through and through.

There was no discussion. As soon as I had told my 'myth', I put on a record of Sibelius's tone-poem *Tapiola*—as an aid to concentration through its appropriately savage, otherworldly atmosphere—and told them I would stop them when the music ended. *Tapiola* lasts about twenty minutes.

These are four (to me) outstanding poems out of many interesting ones; all four authors were fourteen years old. I have not edited them in any way except to correct a few spelling mistakes. As with much children's verse, I am astonished by a spontaneity which I, a professional poet, could not begin to equal. One is tempted to say that children—some at least—create more naturally in poetic form than they do in prose, just as primitive cultures do. What gets in the way of the gift later? And, when all allowance has been made for the power of myth, from what mysterious reaches do those amazing images—the 'picture museum of nothing', 'time tapping itself on the shoulder'—arise? It is interesting that Philip Pryce, in a way characteristic of how the creative imagination works, seems to have hooked out of his memory Neil Armstrong's famous moon-landing phrase, 'one small step for a man, one giant leap for mankind', and shaped it to his own purpose.

[a]   *Sestina*

Farewell, Oh sun, Arcadia's clearest light;
Farewell, Oh pearl, the poor man's plenteous treasure;
Farewell, Oh golden staff, the weak man's might;
Farewell, Oh joy, the joyful's only pleasure;
Wisdom, farewell, the skilless man's direction;
Farewell, with thee farewell, all our affection.

For what place now is left for our affection,
Now that of purest lamp is quenched the light
Which to our dark'ned minds was best direction?
Now that the mine is lost of all our treasure;
Now death hath swallowed up our worldly pleasure,
We orphans made, void of all public might!

Orphans, indeed, deprived of father's might,
For he our father was in all affection,
In our well-doing placing all his pleasure,
Still studying how to us to be a light;
As well he was in peace a safest treasure,
In war his wit and word was our direction.

Whence, whence, alas, shall we seek our direction,
When that we fear our hateful neighbour's might,
Who long have gaped to get Arcadian's treasure?
Shall we now find a guide of such affection,
Who for our sakes will think all travail light,
And make his pain to keep us safe his pleasure?

No, no; forever gone is all our pleasure,
For ever wandering from all good direction,
For ever blinded of our clearest light,
For ever lamèd of our surèd might,
For ever banished from well placed affection,
For ever robbed of all our royal treasure.

Let tears for him therefore be all our treasure,
And in our wailing naming him our pleasure;
Let hating of our selves be our affection,
And unto death bend still our thought's direction;
Let us against our selves employ our might,
And putting out our eyes seek we our light.

Farewell, our light; farewell, our spoilèd treasure;
Farewell, our might; farewell, our daunted pleasure;
Farewell, direction; farewell, all affection.

[b] D. M. THOMAS

The Journey

Mother, hear the wind keening over the Goss Moor,
Tregeagle's sighs, emptying the bottomless Dozmare
Pool. Seeing the world again begins to bore
You. You rub seized joints. I ask you how you are
And the wind fails to force the car
Off the A30. Yes, it is good of me to drive so far,

For one almost as old and bald as Dozmare,
Her life, apart from me, featureless as Goss Moor.
I compute how far
We have to go: seven hours. She who bore
Me is pressed, small, while the decimal nines are
Flickering into noughts, back into the car,

As I was, waiting. I ask how you are;
Must I wind down the window a shade, raise the car-
Heater? It is wrinkled Tregeagle emptying the Dozmare
Pool in you, discomfort, pain, that never fall far
Before rising to the same level. Your harpings bore
Me like this incessant wind over the Goss Moor.

And I cannot look sideways in the car,
It is too painful to see how shrunken you are,
Tacitly, since last the Goss Moor
Shot past us, and hidden Dozmare;
Three thousand miles on the gauge since I came so far
To fetch you. That January day you bore

Me, did the journey feel so far?
Image of starry countdowns that move and bore
Us, I dice with the petrol countdown, see if the car
Will reach the next pump, past Bodmin Moor.
You rest trustful in my omniscience. Old Dozmare
Mother, what strange things and what strangers we are.

I know these three weeks you will bore
Me. I don't read your letters when you are far
Away, those cheerful comforting lies. So; till you are
Dead, as something wants, and, dead, I drive this car
Or the next, for the last time up through the moor
That rose when Dozmare was sea, and sees the end of
    Dozmare.

I help you struggle from the car, to a moorstone. You bore
Your own small Dozmare in thin soil. For we are water and
    moor,
And far journeyers together. Whatever else we are.

One kind of crossing which occurs constantly is of poetic
forms. The form of every poem is unique, yet at the same time
is in a relationship with the forms of countless other poems. The
relationship is particularly close when the poet chooses one of
the traditional fixed forms, such as the sonnet.

The sestina is the most intricate form of an age of metrical
intricacy, twelfth-century Provence. The same end-words must
recur in each of the six six-lined stanzas, and always in a differ-
ent order. The six recurring words are finally compressed into a
half-stanza. An additional complication is that the end-words
may not be permutated at will but in a decreed order. Sidney has
kept strictly to this order, and has created (and solved) further
problems for himself by introducing rhyme, which was not
customary in the Provençal sestina. In *The Journey* I break the
rules by not keeping to the established order, though the end-
words never recur in the same place in the stanza.

I chose to write in this (slightly modified) form because I hoped that its repetitiveness would reflect the tedium of the long-distance journey and—more important—the baffled nature of a relationship which subsists on nothing but blind blood-love and which has no future except death. The extreme discipline of such forms can also help to control overpowering emotion. Dylan Thomas used the even more restrictive villanelle to express grief for his dying father in *Do not go gentle into that good night*. 'The fascination of what's difficult' (Yeats's phrase) is another important reason why these intricate forms continue to live.

[a]   *Sonnet*

Methought I saw my late espoused Saint
   Brought to me like *Alcestis* from the grave,
   Whom *Jove*'s great Son to her glad Husband gave,
   Rescu'd from death by force though pale and faint.
Mine as whom washt from spot of child-bed taint,
   Purification in the old Law did save,
   And such, as yet once more I trust to have
   Full sight of her in Heaven without restraint,
Came vested all in white, pure as her mind:
   Her face was veil'd, yet to my fancied sight,
   Love, sweetness, goodness, in her person shin'd
So clear, as in no face with more delight.
   But O as to embrace me she enclin'd
   I wak'd, she fled, and day brought back my night.

————————

[b] WILLIAM WORDSWORTH

                             Sonnet

Surprised by joy—impatient as the Wind
I turned to share the transport—Oh! with whom
But Thee, deep buried in the silent tomb,
That spot which no vicissitude can find?
Love, faithful love, recalled thee to my mind—
But how could I forget thee? Through what power,
Even for the least division of an hour,
Have I been so beguiled as to be blind
To my most grievous loss!—That thought's return
Was the worst pang that sorrow ever bore,
Save one, one only, when I stood forlorn,
Knowing my heart's best treasure was no more;
That neither present time, nor years unborn
Could to my sight that heavenly face restore.

Milton's sonnet about his second wife, Katherine, and Words-worth's about his second daughter, Catherine, are strikingly alike. Wordsworth must have had the earlier sonnet in mind. He chooses the same, two-rhyme pattern for the sestet, and unifies it further by linking the rhymes through assonance, just as Milton does: 'unborn/restore', 'enclin'd/night'. His octave differs only in lines 6 and 7. Important words, 'more', 'sight', 'face', 'love', and the poignant 'O', are echoes of Milton. Yet the impressive similarity is swallowed up in their utter originality and power. Wordsworth's begins, in a sense, where Milton's ends: with the renewed knowledge of loss. Worse than that, with the intolerable knowledge that he had for a time forgotten his child, lost even to loss. Milton's sonnet is full of his dead wife's livingness, supporting his vision by calling up both Christian and pagan images of resurrection and paradise. (Alcestis is another Euridice, but *fully* rescued from death by Heracles.) And yet, I feel, Catherine's absence is more charged with indestructible human life and love than is Katherine's presence.

Part IV

white song, black ink

poems of oral and recorded cultures

It is right to preface this section with a note of caution. If human beings were clones, all alike, and all undergoing exactly the same experiences, a direct comparison between a 'primitive' and a 'civilized' poem would be possible. Fortunately that is not so. I have grouped poems which seem to me to have a lot in common, in theme or mood or both; but all experiences are unique and so are poets' reactions to them and their ways of organizing experience into art. To underline the caution, I have selected as my first pairing poems which, while they have an emotion in common—a mother's love for a newly born child— are otherwise violently different, in that one mother will watch her child grow up and the other must see it taken away.

Moreover, *any* two cultures will differ, in their life and their art; and the division I have made between oral and recorded is to some extent arbitrary. I hope it goes without saying that by 'primitive' I do not mean unintelligent, and by 'civilized' I do not mean possessing civilized values. Finally, the fact that many of the oral poems are translations will prevent a complete study of form and technique.

Having made these cautionary remarks, I believe that, if we do not draw conclusions from any single grouping but wait until we have read and studied them all, we can learn something about the differences and resemblances between the poetry of oral and recorded cultures—and therefore about poetry itself, those elements of it which may change and those which may be timeless. To help us draw our conclusions, here are some of the questions we might ask: Across the great cultural divides, is poetry inspired by basically the same *kind* of experience? Is the poet's individuality, as against his sense of community, more evident in recorded poetry? Is the intention of oral and recorded poetry different? Does Coleridge's much-approved definition of the poetic imagination—'a more than usual state of emotion with more than usual order'—apply equally well to 'primitive' poetry? Are the imagination's primary elements, passion and intellect, equally well balanced in both? Does oral poetry employ imagery, metaphor, echoism, etc., in similar ways to the modern professional poet?

For those who wish to explore further the poetry of primitive societies, the following anthologies are recommended: *The Unwritten Song*, ed. Willard R. Trask (Cape, 1969); *American Indian Prose and Poetry*, ed. Margot Astrov (New York, Putnam, 1962); and *The Magic Word*, ed. William Brandon (New York, Morrow, 1971).

43[a] ⟨DIDINGA or LANGO, Uganda⟩

A Mother to Her First-born

Speak to me, child of my heart.
Speak to me with your eyes, your round, laughing eyes,
Wet and shining as Lupeyo's bull-calf.

Speak to me, little one,
Clutching my breast with your hand,
So strong and firm for all its littleness.
It will be the hand of a warrior, my son,
A hand that will gladden your father.
See how eagerly it fastens on me:
It thinks already of a spear:
It quivers as at the throwing of a spear.
O son, you will have a warrior's name and be a leader of men.
And your sons, and your sons' sons, will remember you long
    after you have slipped into the darkness.
But I, I shall always remember your hand clutching me so.
I shall recall how you lay in my arms,
And looked at me so, and so,
And how your tiny hands played with my bosom.
And when they name you great warrior, then will my eyes
    be wet with remembering.

And how shall we name you, little warrior?
See, let us play at naming.
It will not be a name of despisal, for you are my first-born.
Not as Nawal's son is named will you be named.
Our gods will be kinder to you than theirs.
Must we call you 'Insolence' or 'Worthless One'?
Shall you be named, like a child of ill fortune, after the
    dung of cattle?

Our gods need no cheating, my child:
They wish you no ill.
They have washed your body and clothed it with beauty.
They have set a fire in your eyes.
And the little, puckering ridges of your brow—
Are they not the seal of their finger-prints when they
      fashioned you?
They have given you beauty and strength, child of my heart,
And wisdom is already shining in your eyes,
And laughter.

So how shall we name you, little one?
Are you your father's father, or his brother, or yet another?
Whose spirit is it that is in you, little warrior?
Whose spear-hand tightens round my breast?
Who lives in you and quickens to life, like last year's melon
      seed?
Are you silent, then?
But your eyes are thinking, thinking, and glowing like the
      eyes of a leopard in a thicket.
Well, let be.
At the day of naming you will tell us.

O my child, now indeed I am happy.
Now indeed I am a wife—
No more a bride, but a Mother-of-one.

Be splendid and magnificent, child of desire.
Be proud, as I am proud.
Be happy, as I am happy.
Be loved, as now I am loved.
Child, child, child, love I have had from my man.
But now, only now, have I the fullness of love.
Now, only now, am I his wife and the mother of his first-
      born.
His soul is safe in your keeping, my child, and it was I, I, I,
      who have made you.
Therefore am I loved.
Therefore am I happy.
Therefore am I a wife.
Therefore have I great honour.

You will tend his shrine when he is gone.
With sacrifice and oblation you will recall his name year by
    year.
He will live in your prayers, my child,
And there will be no more death for him, but everlasting
    life springing from your loins.
You are his shield and spear, his hope and redemption from
    the dead.
Through you he will be reborn, as the saplings in the Spring.
And I, I am the mother of his first-born.
Sleep, child of beauty and courage and fulfilment, sleep.
I am content.

[b] ANNE SEXTON

Unknown Girl in the Maternity Ward

Child, the current of your breath is six days long.
You lie, a small knuckle on my white bed;
lie, fisted like a snail, so small and strong
at my breast. Your lips are animals; you are fed
with love. At first hunger is not wrong.
The nurses nod their caps; you are shepherded
down starch halls with the other unnested throng
in wheeling baskets. You tip like a cup; your head
moving to my touch. You sense the way we belong.
But this is an institution bed.
You will not know me very long.

The doctors are enamel. They want to know
The facts. They guess about the man who left me,
some pendulum soul, going the way men go
and leave you full of child. But our case history
stays blank. All I did was let you grow.
Now we are here for all the ward to see.
They thought I was strange, although
I never spoke a word. I burst empty
of you, letting you learn how the air is so.
The doctors chart the riddle they ask of me
And I turn my head away. I do not know.

Yours is the only face I recognize.
Bone at my bone, you drink my answers in.
Six times a day I prize
your need, the animals of your lips, your skin
growing warm and plump. I see your eyes
lifting their tents. They are blue stones, they begin
to outgrow their moss. You blink in surprise
And I wonder what you can see, my funny kin,
as you trouble my silence. I am a shelter of lies
Should I learn to speak again, or hopeless in
such sanity will I touch some face I recognize?

Down the hall the baskets start back. My arms
fit you like a sleeve, they hold
catkins of your willows, the wild bee farms
of your nerves, each muscle and fold
of your first days. Your old man's face disarms
the nurses. But the doctors return to scold
me. I speak. It is you my silence harms.
I should have known; I should have told
them something to write down. My voice alarms
my throat. 'Name of father—none.' I hold
you and name you bastard in my arms.

And now that's that. There is nothing more
that I can say or lose.
Others have traded life before
and could not speak. I tighten to refuse
your owling eyes, my fragile visitor.
I touch your cheeks, like flowers. You bruise
against me. We unlearn. I am a shore
Rocking you off. You break from me. I choose
your only way, my small inheritor
and hand you off, trembling the selves we lose.
Go child, who is my sin and nothing more.

━━━━◇━━━━

Anne Sexton has said that she wrote her poem as a result of
meeting such a mother while in a mental home. Her own guilt
at having (unintentionally) deserted her children by being sick
fused with the experience related to her by the 'unknown girl'.

44[a] ⟨PAPAGO, American Indian⟩

Two Dream Songs

1

Where the mountain crosses,
On top of the mountain,
   I do not myself know where,
I wandered where my mind and my heart
   seemed to be lost.
I wandered away.

2

There is a white shell mountain in the ocean
Rising half out of the water.
Green scum floats on the water
And the mountain turns around.

[b] JOHN DONNE

from *Elegy XVI*

When I am gone, dream me some happiness,
Nor let thy looks our long hid love confess,
Nor praise, nor dispraise me, nor bless nor curse
Openly love's force, nor in bed fright thy Nurse
With midnight's startings, crying out, oh, oh
Nurse, o my love is slain, I saw him go
O'er the white Alps alone; I saw him I,
Assail'd, fight, taken, stabb'd, bleed, fall, and die.
Augur me better chance, except dread *Jove*
Think it enough for me to have had thy love.

from *Rejoice in the Lamb*

For I prophecy that men will learn the use of their knees.
For everything that can be done in that posture (upon
the knees) is better so done than otherwise.
For I prophecy that they will understand the blessing
and virtue of the rain.
For rain is exceedingly good for the human body.
For it is good therefore to have flat roofs to the houses,
as of old.
For it is good to let the rain come upon the naked body
unto purity and refreshment.

'Many (American) Indian songs are intended to exert a strong
mental influence, and dream songs are supposed to have this
power in greater degree than any others. The supernatural is
very real to the Indian. He puts himself in communication with
it by fasting or by physical suffering. While his body is thus
subordinated to the mind a song occurs to him. In after years
he believes that by singing this song he can recall the condition
under which it came to him—a condition of direct communi-
cation with the supernatural.'

FRANCES DENSMORE: *Chippewa Music*
(1913, repr. NY, Plenum, 1971)

'When I was about eight years old, my father once made an
image of a mountain out of cactus ribs covered with white cloth.
He had dreamed about this mountain and this is the song he
made:

[There is a white shell mountain. . . .]

The song is short because we know so much. We can understand
how tall and white the mountain was, and that white shell is
something precious, such as the handsome men of old used to
have for their necklaces, and it would shine all across the earth

as they walked. We understand that as that mountain turns, it draws the clouds and the birds until all float around it.'

R. UNDERHILL: *The Autobiography of a Papago Woman*
(1936; repr. NY, Kraus)

There are no dream-songs in English poetry; but I have selected two passages which seem to me to have something of the same mixture of simplicity and symbolic mystery: a mixture which reminds me of some magnificent words by the Elizabethan George Chapman: 'Obscurity in affection of words, & indigested conceits, is pedantical and childish; but where it shroudeth it self in the heart of his subject, uttered with fitness of figure, and expressive epithets; with that darkness will I still labour to be shadowed.'

45[a] ⟨AZTEC⟩

Love Song

I know not whether thou hast been absent:
I lie down with thee, I rise up with thee,
In my dreams thou art with me.
If my eardrops tremble in my ears,
I know it is thou moving within my heart.

––––––––––––

[b] WILLIAM SHAKESPEARE

Sonnet 97

How like a winter hath my absence been
From thee, the pleasure of the fleeting year!
What freezings have I felt, what dark days seen!
What old December's bareness every where!
And yet this time remov'd was summer's time;
The teeming autumn, big with rich increase,
Bearing the wanton burden of the prime,
Like widow'd wombs after their lords' decease:
Yet this abundant issue seem'd to me
But hope of orphans and unfather'd fruit;
For summer and his pleasures wait on thee,
And, thou away, the very birds are mute;
    Of, if they sing, 'tis with so dull a cheer,
    That leaves look pale, dreading the winter's near.

––––––––––––

The song was obtained from the lips of an Indian girl in the Sierra of Tamaulipas.

Shakespeare's sonnets were not primarily intended for publication, but were read in manuscript by a circle of intimates, including presumably the young man to whom most of the sonnets are addressed. There is, in this reticence, the understandable feeling that a love poem is private. No doubt the Aztec song was also personal rather than tribal.

46[a] ⟨CHEROKEE, American Indian⟩

A Spell to Destroy Life

Listen!
  Now I have come to step over your soul
    (I know your clan)
    (I know your name)
    (I have stolen your spit and buried it under earth)
  I bury your soul under earth
  I cover you over with black rock
  I cover you over with black cloth
  I cover you over with black slabs
  You disappear forever

  Your path leads to the
                Black Coffin
                in the hills of the Darkening Land
  So let it be for you

  The clay of the hills covers you
  The black clay of the Darkening Land

  Your soul fades away

  It becomes blue

  When darkness comes your spirit shrivels and dwindles
                  to disappear forever

Listen!

The Apparition

When by thy scorn, O murd'ress I am dead,
   And that thou thinkst thee free
From all solicitatión from me,
Then shall my ghost come to thy bed,
And thee, fain'd vestal, in worse arms shall see;
Then thy sick taper will begin to wink,
And he, whose thou art then, being tir'd before,
Will, if thou stir, or pinch to wake him, think
   Thou call'st for more,
And in false sleep will from thee shrink,
And then poor Aspen wretch, neglected thou
Bath'd in a cold quicksilver sweat wilt lie
   A verier ghost than I;
What I will say, I will not tell thee now,
Lest that preserve thee; and since my love is spent,
I had rather thou shouldst painfully repent,
Than by my threat'nings rest still innocent.

'The device of rhyme seems not to have been used by the most cultivated Americans of pre-Columbian times ... Nor were there any certain stanza forms except such as were brought about by the repetition of phrases. The outstanding feature of American Indian verse construction comes from parallel phrasing, or, let us say, repetition with an increment, which gives an effect not of rhyming sounds but of rhyming thoughts.'

HERBERT J. SPINDEN: *Songs of the Tewa* (New York, 1933)

The dread Cherokee incantation was possessed in the late nineteenth century by a medicine-man called A'yunini (Swimmer). We do not know if, or how often, he used it, nor with what success. Donne's incantation against a scornful mistress does not go quite as far, and perhaps it is more literary than literal; but it is flesh-creeping enough.

Passion Spent

At the core of my being, in the pale light of early dawn,
   Your spear advances in flaming ardor.

   Now it has withdrawn.

Our bodies are like the tiny leaved mint in fragrance;
They have been anointed with the sweet scented sap
      of the wild ginger root,
Gathered on the bold promontory, Hill-of-the-children,
      jutting into the blue reflection of the lagoon,
From the western flank of the mountain called Life-giving-
      creator.
The secluded nook, Land-crab-scuttling-over-the-flowering-
      dell, is our trysting place,
Where the plover twitters as it snatches small fry
      from the brook, Clamoring-waters.
Oh, deep is our rapture in our secret retreat,
While ever the great temple—
Primordial-abyss-within-the-dark-rim-of-the-rock-base-of-the-
      world, the flaming body of woman—
Gleams in the flickering light of moving torches;
A temple consecrated to the two thighs of the Earth-mother
Ever bringing forth children into this world of light.

   Behold! The divine goddess!

   O Urgent desire—
   Assuaged in the cup-of-life!
O Adored Cup-of-life—
   Enfolding the flame of desire!
O Ecstasy!

   Rapturous is the union of the gods!

from *Ovid's Banquet of Sense*

In a loose robe of Tinsel forth she came,
Nothing but it betwixt her nakedness
And envious light. The downward burning flame
Of her rich hair did threaten new access
    Of venturous *Phaëton* to scorch the fields:
And thus to bathing came our Poet's Goddess,
    Her handmaids bearing all things pleasure yields
To such a service; Odours most delighted,
And purest linen which her looks had whited.

Then cast she off her robe, and stood upright,
As lightning breaks out of a labouring cloud;
Or as the Morning heaven casts off the Night,
Or as that heaven cast off it self, and show'd
    Heaven's upper light, to which the brightest day
Is but a black and melancholy shroud:
    Or as when *Venus* striv'd her sovereign sway
Of charmful beauty, in young Troy's desire,
So stood *Corinna* vanishing her tire.

A soft enflower'd bank embrac'd the fount;
Of *Chloris'* ensigns, an abstracted field;
Where grew Melanthy, great in Bees' account,
Amareus, that precious Balm doth yield,
    Enamel'd Pansies, us'd at Nuptials still,
Diana's arrow, *Cupid's* crimson shield.
    Ope-morn, night-shade, and *Venus'* navel,
Solemn Violets, hanging head as shamed,
And verdant Calaminth, for odour famed;

Sacred Nepenthe, purgative of care,
And sovereign Rumex that doth rancour kill,
Sya, and Hyacinth, that Furies wear,
White and red Jessamines, Merry, Melliphill:
    Fair Crown-imperial, Emperor of Flowers,
Immortal Amaranth, white Aphrodill,
    And cup-like Twillpants, strewed in *Bacchus'* powers,
These cling about this Nature's naked Gem,
To taste her sweets, as Bees do swarm on them.

And now she used the Fount, where *Niobe*,
Tomb'd in her self, pour'd her lost soul in tears
Upon the bosom of this Roman *Phoebe*;
Who, bath'd and Odour'd, her bright limbs she rears,
   And drying her on that disparent ground,
Her Lute she takes t'enamour heavenly ears,
   And try if with her voice's vital sound
She could warm life through those cold statues spread,
And cheer the Dame that wept when she was dead.

And thus she sung, all naked as she sat,
Laying the happy Lute upon her thigh,
Not thinking any near to wonder at
The bliss of her sweet breasts' divinity.

disparent: clear.

---

[c] GEORGE CHAPMAN

from *A Hymn to Hymen*

Gentle, O Gentle *Hymen*, be not then
Cruel, That kindest art to Maids, and Men;
These two, One Twin are; and their mutual bliss,
Not in thy beams, but in thy Bosom is.
Nor can their hands fast, their hearts' joys make sweet;
Their hearts, in breasts are; and their Breasts must meet.
Let there be Peace, yet Murmur: and that noise
Beget of peace the Nuptial battle's joys.
Let Peace grow cruel, and take wrack of all,
The war's delay brought thy full Festival.
Hark, hark, O now the sweet Twin murmur sounds;
Hymen is come, and all his heat abounds;
Shut all Doors; None, but *Hymen*'s lights advance;
No sound stir, let dumb Joy enjoy a trance.
Sing, sing a Rapture to all Nuptial ears,
Bright *Hymen*'s Torches drunk up *Parcae*'s tears.

Note. 'Parcae': the Fates.

178

The passage from *Ovid's Banquet of Sense* is a love poem to life-giving womanhood, nature—and the English language, at a time when nothing was impossible to it. In its colour and delighted fleshly excess, it is like a Rubens painting. This analogy calls to mind a recent (1973) series of BBC television programmes, in which the art critic John Berger presented the theory that the history of the nude, in European painting, is the story of man's lust to possess objects; the nude woman, he suggested, was rarely seen as a person, but rather as a desirable *thing* voyeuristically possessed by the painting's owner. While I do not necessarily agree with this—indeed, I don't know enough about the history of European art to be able to judge—it *is* interesting that in the last lines of Chapman's description we are made aware that someone is watching the naked Corinna in secret. Ostensibly this viewer is the Roman poet Ovid; but the real viewer is Chapman—is myself as reader.

Hymn to Hymen, on the nuptials of Elizabeth, daughter of James I, is an exact English parallel to the Polynesian marriage-poem.

Song of the Sky Loom

Oh our Mother the Earth, oh our Father the Sky,
Your children are we, and with tired backs
We bring you the gifts that you love.
Then weave for us a garment of brightness;
May the warp be the white light of morning,
May the weft be the red light of evening,
May the fringes be the falling rain,
May the border be the standing rainbow.
Thus weave for us a garment of brightness
That we may walk fittingly where birds sing,
That we may walk fittingly where grass is green,
Oh our Mother the Earth, oh our Father the Sky!

---

[b] GERARD MANLEY HOPKINS

Pied Beauty

Glory be to God for dappled things—
    For skies of couple-colour as a brinded cow;
      For rose-moles all in stipple upon trout that swim;
Fresh-firecoal chestnut-falls; finches' wings;
    Landscape plotted and pieced—fold, fallow, and plough;
      And áll trádes, their gear and tackle and trim.
All things counter, original, spare, strange:
    Whatever is fickle, freckled (who knows how?)
      With swift, slow; sweet, sour; adazzle, dim;
He fathers-forth whose beauty is past change:
                         Praise him.

'More often than not, the singer aims with the chanted word
to exert a strong influence and to bring about a change, either
in himself or in nature or in his fellow beings. By narrating the
story of origin, he endeavours to influence the universe and to

strengthen the failing power of the supernatural beings. He relates the myth of creation, ceremonially, in order to save the world from death and destruction and to keep alive the primeval spirit of the sacred beginning. Above all, it seems that the word, both in song and in tale, was meant to maintain and to prolong the individual life in some way or other—that is, to cure, to heal, to ward off evil, and to frustrate death. Healing songs, and songs intended to support the powers of germination and of growth in all their manifestations, fairly outnumber all other songs of the American Indian.'

MARGOT ASTROV: *American Indian Prose and Poetry*

The sky loom refers to the small desert rain: like wandering looms the rainshowers hang from the sky.

49[a] ⟨LANGO, Uganda⟩

from *The Rain-making Ceremony*

Recitative	*Response*
We overcome this wind.	We overcome.
We desire the rain to fall, that it be poured in showers quickly.	Be poured.
Ah! thou rain, I adjure thee fall. If thou rainest, it is well.	It is well.
A drizzling confusion.	Confusion.
If it rains and our food ripens, it is well.	It is well.
If the children rejoice, it is well.	It is well.
If it rains, it is well. If our women rejoice, it is well	It is well.
If the young men sing, it is well.	It is well.
A drizzling confusion.	Confusion.
If our grain ripens, it is well.	It is well.
If our women rejoice.	It is well.
If the children rejoice.	It is well.
If the young men sing.	It is well.
If the aged rejoice.	It is well.
An overflowing in the granary.	Overflowing.
May our grain fill the granaries.	May it fill.
A torrent in flow.	A torrent.
If the wind veers to the south, it is well.	It is well.
If the rain veers to the south, it is well.	It is well.

Note. 'overcome this wind': the dry season wind is easterly, and the rains come when the wind veers to the south.

'Thou art indeed just'

Thou art indeed just, Lord, if I contend
With thee; but, sir, so what I plead is just.
Why do sinners' ways prosper? and why must
Disappointment all I endeavour end?
　　Wert thou my enemy, O thou my friend,
How wouldst thou worse, I wonder, than thou dost
Defeat, thwart me? Oh, the sots and thralls of lust
Do in spare hours more thrive than I that spend,
Sir, life upon thy cause. See, banks and brakes
Now, leavèd how thick! lacèd they are again
With fretty chervil, look, and fresh wind shakes
Them; birds build—but not I build; no, but strain,
Time's eunuch, and not breed one work that wakes.
Mine, O thou lord of life, send my roots rain.

The Rain-Making Ceremony: compare what has been said on the characteristic 'rhyming-thoughts' in American Indian poetry.

　　Hopkins's cry for spiritual rain was written when many years of self-denying service as a Jesuit priest had drained his energies. 'I am a eunuch,' he wrote to his friend Robert Bridges, 'but it is for the kingdom of heaven's sake.'

50[a] ⟨SEA DYAK, Borneo⟩

Evening Quietness

The cricket
sings its evening song,
telling the eye of day
has sunk and gone.

The young ngingit
trumpets
from the waving branch,
for the sun
has sunk
in the glowing west.

The young otter
has ceased its gambols,
chasing its prey
on the ripples of the pebbly beach.

The young mouse deer
now slinks away
for its search for cane,
in the deserted garden.

The chicks
with noisy chirp
have found their coop.

The great white fowls
side by side
have sought their roost.

The great fat pig
grunting
has sought its sty.

The jutting poles
tremble
with the weight of speckled fowl.

The sky
is serried and painted,
like the fringe
of the petangan head-dress.

The sky
is oval and white,
like a plate
of a banquet-house.

The sky
is dark and red,
like the tail
of the perching hornbill.

The sky
is spotted and barred,
like the scales
of the mengkarong lizard.

The sky
is parded and red,
like the painted skin
of the tree leopard.

Black cloud-piles
slowly sail
and roll away.

The yellow star
now twinkles
near the circle
of the moon.

The Pleiads, one by one,
shine out
in their wonted place.

The three stars
proudly sail
chasing one another.

The evening star
shines beautiful,
like the budding
kenunsong flower.

The Mlanau star
trembles
in the vault of the deep, dark sky.

The star Perdah
pursues its course
on its mighty way.

The verandah grows
dark as though wrapped
in the blantan blanket.

And our house loft,
friend Budi Nsirimbai, grows
dark as though covered
with a paia pakan.

The whole house
trembles buried in gloom.
And now our resin lamps,
friend Nyeni Budi Mejah,
make glowing spots
in the village pathway.

The children
have ceased
their noisy games and quarrels.

The mothers
have ceased to nurse
their latest born.

The widows
have sought the secluded couch
up the low ladder.

The village maids
with giggle and noisy laugh
have sought the cot
in the loft above.

The old men
have ceased to feed
the evening fire.

Note. 'Ngingit': a cicada; its note is heard only a little after sunset.
'The three stars': Orion. 'Paia pakan': a woven blanket.

[**b**] ROBERT FROST

Come In

As I came to the edge of the woods,
Thrush music—hark!
Now if it was dusk outside,
Inside it was dark.

Too dark in the woods for a bird
By sleight of wing
To better its perch for the night,
Though it still could sing.

The last of the light of the sun
That had died in the west
Still lived for one song more
In a thrush's breast.

Far in the pillared dark
Thrush music went—
Almost like a call to come in
To the dark and lament.

But no, I was out for stars:
I would not come in.
I meant not even if asked,
And I hadn't been.

Evening Quietness is part of a sacred chant, *Flowers of the Year*, used by the Sea Dyaks on the occasion of a sacrificial feast to invoke a blessing on the harvest. Scholars from all over the primitive world have attested to the extraordinary powers of memory that are brought to bear in order to preserve such sacred texts unaltered, from generation to generation:

'I know Kabyles who can recite verses through a whole day without repeating themselves and without hesitating. I have several times tested them by making them repeat songs written from their dictation a year or two earlier, and I have never found them making a mistake.' (Africa)

'(Poets) teach their compositions to bands of youths who master every detail of the poem in a single evening. It is then as permanent and unalterable as if it had been set up in type. I had a curious instance of the remarkable verbal memory of the Fijians in a long poem taken down from the lips of an old woman in 1893. The poem had been published by Waterhouse twenty-seven years earlier, and on comparison only one verbal discrepancy between the two versions was found.'

(Quoted by Willard R. Trask: *The Unwritten Song.*)

In Brazil, we hear of youths strengthening their memories by eating certain plants.

Get up and Bar the Door

It fell about the Martinmas time,
    And a gay time it was then,
When our goodwife got puddings to make,
    And she's boild them in the pan.

The wind sae cauld blew south and north,
    And blew into the floor;
Quoth our goodman to our goodwife,
    'Gae out and bar the door.'

'My hand is in my hussyfskap,
    Goodman, as ye may see;
An it should nae be barrd this hundred year,
    It's no be barrd for me.'

They made a paction tween them twa,
    They made it firm and sure,
That the first word whaeer shoud speak,
    Shoud rise and bar the door.

Then by there came two gentlemen,
    At twelve o clock at night,
And they could neither see house nor hall,
    Nor coal nor candle-light.

'Now whether is this a rich man's house,
    Or whether is it a poor?'
But neer a word wad ane o them speak,
    For barring of the door.

And first they ate the white puddings,
    And then they ate the black;
Tho muckle thought the goodwife to hersel,
    Yet neer a word she spake.

Then said the one unto the other,
    'Here, man, tak ye my knife;
Do ye tak aff the auld man's beard,
    And I'll kiss the goodwife.'

'But there's nae water in the house,
  And what shall we do than?'
'What ails ye at the pudding-broo,
  That boils into the pan?'

O up then started our goodman,
  An angry man was he:
'Will ye kiss my wife before my een,
  And scad me wi pudding-bree?'

Then up and started our goodwife,
  Gied three skips on the floor:
'Goodman, you've spoken the foremost word,
  Get up and bar the door.'

———————

[**b**] CHARLES CAUSLEY

'Mother, get up, unbar the door'

Mother, get up, unbar the door,
Throw wide the window-pane,
I see a man stand all covered in sand
Outside in Vicarage Lane.

His body is shot with seventy stars,
His face is cold as Cain,
His coat is a crust of desert dust
And he comes from Alamein.

He has not felt the flaking frost,
He has not felt the rain,
And not one blow of the burning snow
Since the night that he was slain.

O mother, in your husband's arms
Too long now you have lain,
Rise up, my dear, your true-love's here
Upon the peaceful plain.

Though, mother, on your broken brow
Forty long years are lain,
The soldier they slew at twenty-two
Never a one does gain.

I will unlock the fine front-door
And snap the silver chain,
And meek as milk in my skin of silk
I'll ease him of his pain.

My breast has been for years eighteen
As white as Charles's wain,
But now I'm had by a soldier lad
Whistling *Lili Marlene.*

Farewell to Jack, farewell to Jim,
And farewell Mary Jane,
Farewell the good green sisterhood
Knitting at purl and plain.

Go wash the water from your eye,
The bullet from your brain.
I'm drowned as a dove in the tunnel of love
And I'll never come home again.

———————

'Get up and bar the door' is an old Scots song, based on a comic folk-tale. Charles Causley has made notable use of ballad and other popular forms. In this example, he has chosen to provide a strong rhyme-echo; 'pane' in verse 1 is echoed seventeen times, and there is additionally an internal rhyme in the third line of each verse.

The Unquiet Grave

Cold blows the wind to my true love,
    And gently drops the rain,
I never had but one sweetheart,
    And in greenwood she lies slain,
    And in greenwood she lies slain.

I'll do as much for my sweetheart
    As any young man may;
I'll sit and mourn all on her grave
    For a twelvemonth and a day.

When the twelvemonth and one day was past,
    The ghost began to speak;
'Why sittest here all on my grave,
    And will not let me sleep?'

'There's one thing that I want, sweetheart,
    There's one thing that I crave;
And that is a kiss from your lily-white lips—
    Then I'll go from your grave.'

'My breast it is as cold as clay,
    My breath smells earthly strong;
And if you kiss my cold clay lips,
    Your days they won't be long.

'Go fetch me water from the desert,
    And blood from out of a stone;
Go fetch me milk from a fair maid's breast
    That a young man never had known.'

'O down in yonder grove, sweetheart,
    Where you and I would walk,
The first flower that ever I saw
    Is withered to a stalk.

'The stalk is wither'd and dry, sweetheart,
    And the flower will never return;
And since I lost my own sweetheart,
    What can I do but mourn?

'When shall we meet again, sweetheart?
    When shall we meet again?'
'When the oaken leaves that fall from the trees
    Are green and spring up again,
    Are green and spring up again.'

———————

[b] CHARLES CAUSLEY

The Ballad of Charlotte Dymond

Charlotte Dymond, a domestic servant aged eighteen, was murdered near Rowtor Ford on Bodmin Moor on Sunday, 14th April, 1844, by her young man: a crippled farm-hand, Matthew Weeks, aged twenty-two. A stone marks the spot.

It was a Sunday evening
    And in the April rain
That Charlotte went from our house
    And never came home again.

Her shawl of diamond redcloth,
    She wore a yellow gown,
She carried the green gauze handkerchief
    She bought in Bodmin town.

About her throat her necklace
    And in her purse her pay:
The four silver shillings
    She had at Lady Day.

In her purse four shillings
    And in her purse her pride
As she walked out one evening
    Her lover at her side.

Out beyond the marshes
    Where the cattle stand,
With her crippled lover
    Limping at her hand.

Charlotte walked with Matthew
  Through the Sunday mist,
Never saw the razor
  Waiting at his wrist.

Charlotte she was gentle
  But they found her in the flood
Her Sunday beads among the reeds
  Beaming with her blood.

Matthew, where is Charlotte,
  And wherefore has she flown?
For you walked out together
  And now are come alone.

Why do you not answer,
  Stand silent as a tree,
Your Sunday worsted stockings
  All muddied to the knee?

Why do you mend your breast-pleat
  With a rusty needle's thread
And fall with fears and silent tears
  Upon your single bed?

Why do you sit so sadly
  Your face the colour of clay
And with a green gauze handkerchief
  Wipe the sour sweat away?

Has she gone to Blisland
  To seek an easier place,
And is that why your eye won't dry
  And blinds your bleaching face?

'Take me home!' cried Charlotte,
  'I lie here in the pit!
A red rock rests upon my breasts
  And my naked neck is split!'

Her skin was soft as sable
Her eyes were wide as day,
Her hair was blacker than the bog
  That licked her life away.

Her cheeks were made of honey,
    Her throat was made of flame
Where all around the razor
    Had written its red name.

As Matthew turned at Plymouth
    About the tilting Hoe,
The cold and cunning Constable
    Up to him did go:

'I've come to take you, Matthew,
    Unto the Magistrate's door.
Come quiet now, you pretty poor boy,
    And you must know what for.'

'She is as pure,' cried Matthew,
    'As is the early dew,
Her only stain it is the pain
    That round her neck I drew!

She is as guiltless as the day
    She sprang forth from her mother.
The only sin upon her skin
    Is that she loved another.'

They took him off to Bodmin,
    They pulled the prison bell,
They sent him smartly up to Heaven
    And dropped him down to Hell.

All through the granite kingdom
    And on its travelling airs
Ask which of these two lovers
    The most deserves your prayers.

And your steel heart search, Stranger,
    That you may pause and pray
For lovers who come not to bed
    Upon their wedding day,

But lie upon the moorland
    Where stands the sacred snow
Above the breathing river,
    And the salt sea-winds go.

There is a wider range of language and tone in Causley's modern ballad, without undue sacrifice of tragic concentration. Notice, for example, the witty play on words in 'Has she gone to Blisland / To seek an easier place . . .' Blisland is a remote hamlet on Bodmin Moor, and place means 'situation (as a servant)'. Such verbal sophistication, concealed though it is, is not a characteristic of the tragic traditional ballads.

For two other versions of *The Unquiet Grave*, see **26**, p. 98.

Strawberry Fair

[a] Traditional version

As I was agoing to Strawberry Fair,
   Ri-tol-ri-tol, riddle-tol-de-lido,
I saw a fair maiden of beauty rare,
   Tol-de-dee.
I saw a fair maid go selling her ware
As she went on to Strawberry Fair,
   Ri-tol-ri-tol, riddle-tol-de-lido.

O pretty fair maiden, I prithee tell,
My pretty fair maid, what do you sell?
O come tell me truly, my sweet damsel,
As you go on to Strawberry Fair.

O I have a lock that doth lack a key,
O I have a lock, sir, she did say.
If you have a key then come this way
As we go on to Strawberry Fair.

Between us I reckon that when we met
The key to the lock it was well set,
The key to the lock it well did fit
As we went on to Strawberry Fair.

O would that my lock had been a gun,
I'd shoot the blacksmith, for I'm undone,
And wares to carry I now have none
That I should go to Strawberry Fair.

Note. 'Blacksmith': locksmith.

———————

As I was going to Strawberry Fair,
Singing, singing, Butter-cups and Daisies
I met a maiden taking her ware,
      Fol-de-dee!
Her eyes were blue and golden her hair,
As she went on to Strawberry Fair,
  Ri-fol, Ri-fol, Tol-de-riddle-li-do,
  Ri-fol, Ri-fol, Tol-de-riddle-dee.

'Kind Sir, pray pick of my basket!' she said,
  Singing, etc.
'My cherries ripe, or my roses red,
      Fol-de-dee!
My strawberries sweet, I can of them spare,
  As I go on to Strawberry Fair.'
    Ri-fol etc.

Your cherries soon will be wasted away,
  Singing, etc.
Your roses wither and never stay,
      Tol-de-dee!
'Tis not to seek such perishing ware,
That I am tramping to Strawberry Fair.
    Ri-fol etc.

I want to purchase a generous heart,
  Singing, etc.
A tongue that neither is nimble nor tart.
      Tol-de-dee!
An honest mind, but such trifles are rare
I doubt if they're found at Strawberry Fair.
    Ri-fol etc.

The price I offer, my sweet pretty maid
  Singing, etc.
A ring of gold on your finger displayed,
      Tol-de-dee!
So come make over to me your ware,
In church today at Strawberry Fair.
    Ri-fol etc.

Strawberry Fair was first recorded by the Rev. Sabine Baring-Gould, in 1891. So much, in so many fields, is owed to this enormously gifted and energetic man (among other achievements, he was the author of 150 books and fifteen children), that we can forgive his efforts to bowdlerize some of the songs he collected—just in time—from the dying race of illiterate travelling singers on the moors of Devon and Cornwall. In any case, he took the trouble to deposit the authentic texts in the Plymouth City Library. He was a good writer, and it is interesting to compare the poetic merits of his versions and the originals. He wrote of *Strawberry Fair*: 'This song was extremely early, but unsuitable; and I have been constrained to rewrite it. . . . The ballad is sung everywhere in Cornwall and Devon to the same melody. The words are certainly not later than the age of Charles II, and are probably older. They turn on a double entendre which is quite lost—and fortunately so—to half the old fellows who sing the song.'

54[a] ⟨FOLK SONG⟩

'I will give my love an apple'

I will give my love an apple without e'er a core,
I will give my love a house without e'er a door.
I will give my love a palace wherein she may be
And she may unlock it without e'er a key.

My head is the apple without e'er a core,
My mind is the house without e'er a door,
My heart is the palace wherein she may be
And she may unlock it without e'er a key.

I will give my love a cherry without e'er a stone,
I will give my love a chick without e'er a bone,
I will give my love a ring, not a rent to be seen,
I will get my love children without any crying.

When the cherry's in blossom there's never no stone,
When the chick's in the womb there's never no bone,
And when they're rinning running not a rent to be seen,
And when they're child-making they're seldom crying.

———

[b] CHRISTOPHER MARLOWE

The Passionate Shepherd to his Love

Come live with me, and be my love,
And we will all the pleasures prove,
That valleys, groves, hills and fields,
Woods, or steepy mountain yields.

And we will sit upon the Rocks,
Seeing the Shepherds feed their flocks,
By shallow Rivers, to whose falls,
Melodious birds sing Madrigals.

And I will make thee beds of Roses,
And a thousand fragrant posies,
A cap of flowers, and a kirtle,
Embroidered all with leaves of Myrtle.

A gown made of the finest wool,
Which from our pretty Lambs we pull,
Fair lined slippers for the cold:
With buckles of the purest gold.

A belt of straw, and Ivy buds,
With Coral clasps and Amber studs,
And if these pleasures may thee move,
Come live with me, and be my love.

The Shepherds' Swains shall dance & sing,
For thy delight each May-morning,
If these delights thy mind may move,
Then live with me, and be my love.

———◇———

The folk-song was recorded at Sherborne, 1906. James Reeves (*The Everlasting Circle*, Heinemann, 1960, p. 161) refers to a ballad, *Captain Wedderburn's Courtship*, and a fifteenth-century song, which are very similar. The theme of riddling courtships is common in ballad and folk-song, and may have evolved from ancient courtship rituals in which the groom had to undergo various ordeals to test his character and resourcefulness before he could claim his bride. The motivation of Marlowe's shepherd seems less complex.

55[a] ⟨FOLK SONG⟩

The Everlasting Circle

All in the greenwood there growèd a tree,
So fine a tree as you ever did see
And the green leaves flourished around around around
And the green leaves flourished around,

And all on this tree there growèd a branch,
So fine a branch as you ever did see
And the branch was on the tree
And the tree was in the wood
And the green leaves flourished . . .

And all on this branch there growèd a spray,
So fine a spray as you ever did see
And the spray was on the branch,
And the branch . . .

And all on this spray there was a fine nest,
So fine a nest as you ever did see
And the nest was on the spray
And the spray . . .

And all in this nest there was laid an egg . . .

And all in this egg there was a golden yolk . . .

And all in this yolk there was a gay bird . . .

And all on this bird there was a fine feather . . .

And out of this feather was made a fine bed . . .

And all on this bed a lad did lie . . .

And all with this lad a maiden she did sleep . . .

And all in this maiden a baby was made . . .

And out of this baby a boy he did grow . . .

And the boy he did lay in the ground an acorn . . .

And out of this acorn did grow a great tree.

Warning to Children

Children, if you dare to think
Of the greatness, rareness, muchness,
Fewness of this precious only
Endless world in which you say
You live, you think of things like this:
Blocks of slate enclosing dappled
Red and green, enclosing tawny
Yellow nets, enclosing white
And black acres of dominoes,
Where a neat brown paper parcel
Tempts you to untie the string.
In the parcel a small island,
On the island a large tree,
On the tree a husky fruit.
Strip the husk and pare the rind off:
In the kernel you will see
Blocks of slate enclosed by dappled
Red and green, enclosed by tawny
Yellow nets, enclosed by white
And black acres of dominoes,
Where the same brown paper parcel—
Children, leave the string alone!
For who dares undo the parcel
Finds himself at once inside it,
On the island, in the fruit,
Blocks of slate about his head,
Finds himself enclosed by dappled
Green and red, enclosed by black
And white acres of dominoes,
With the same brown paper parcel
Still unopened on his knee.
And, if he then should dare to think
Of the fewness, muchness, rareness,
Greatness of this endless only
Precious world in which he says
He lives—he then unties the string.

Spell of Creation

Within the flower there lies a seed,
Within the seed there springs a tree,
Within the tree there spreads a wood.

In the wood there burns a fire,
And in the fire there melts a stone,
Within the stone a ring of iron.

Within the ring there lies an O
Within the O there looks an eye,
In the eye there swims a sea,

And in the sea reflected sky,
And in the sky there shines the sun,
Within the sun a bird of gold.

Within the bird there beats a heart,
And from the heart there flows a song,
And in the song there sings a word.

In the word there speaks a world,
A world of joy, a world of grief,
From joy and grief there springs my love.

Oh love, my love, there springs a world,
And on the world there shines a sun
And in the sun there burns a fire,

Within the fire consumes my heart
And in my heart there beats a bird,
And in the bird there wakes an eye,

Within the eye, earth, sea and sky,
Earth, sky and sea within an O
Lie like the seed within the flower.

This version of the folk-song, which, according to James Reeves in *The Everlasting Circle* (p. 102), is the only one where the 'circle' is completed, was taken down by Baring-Gould at Lew Down, Devon, around the end of the last century. Variations on this theme are numerous and occur in many languages. From *On Ilkla Moor Bah' tat* to Eliot's *Four Quartets*—'Through the unknown, remembered gate / When the last of earth left to discover / Is that which was the beginning'—folk-song and poetry, all literature, has a fascination with this idea.

Part V

ghost images

poems on poetry

What Metre Is

it is a matter
of counting (five
syllables in the first line, four
in the second) and

so on. Or we can change to
seven words in the first line
six in the second. Is
that arbitrary?

Prose is another possibility. There could be three sentences in
the stanza. This would be an example of that.

Which (on the other hand)
we could lay out
by a letter count, as (this by the way is
free verse, without metre)

'pro
se is another possib
ility. There could be th
ree sent
ences in the st
anza. This would be an exam
ple of that.' I mean
it is a matter
of mathematics. Intervals between
the words, three to
a line is the
rule here. It results
in the same as
having words, four to
a line. In the
mind of the poet,
though, it makes a
difference. White spaces
(now it is two spaces) are

just articulation,
space, words
(now it
is one)

mean
something

(now
it
is
words) and

no it is
not
music either. Internal
rhyming (though sometimes
the kernel of new ideas) is
a matter of timing.

The same is true for
rhythm, the beat
(two to a line
it is here)

only becomes like a rhythm when
as here it moves with a regular
dactyl or two to a line. If

slow now spondees
make lines move, stiff

rhythm is metre (in dactyls again) but
rhythm is usually not
like this. In a word

it can escalate
drop

do as it pleases
move freely
(look out, I'm coming)

stop
at a stop

and so on. Assonance
that semblance
(except in Owen)
a, when

it works, echo
of awkwardness is O.K.

but not for me: nor is lively
alliteration

leaping
long lean and allusive
through low lines. It
becomes a matter
of going back
to metre, ending w

ith its mos
t irrit
ating (perhaps) manif
estation thi
s inarticul
ate mechanical stu
tter. It is the voi
ce of the type-wr
iter. It is the abdic
ation of insp

iration. I li
ke it. It i
s the logica

l exp
ression o
f itsel
f.

Besides its usefulness as a mnemonic, this witty, light-hearted poem, by one of the most technically accomplished poets writing today, raises some interesting questions about form. Could he be serious when he says that to have four words or three spaces to a line is the same, yet to the poet it makes a difference? If so, how? And his final typewriter-stutter, with its excellent definition of form—'It i/s the logica/l exp/ression o/f itsel/f'—may make us wonder whether, in a computerized society of the future, poetry can (and perhaps whether it should) retain any roots in traditional form.

from *An Ode: Of Wit*

'Tis not to force some lifeless Verses meet
  With their five gouty feet.
All everywhere, like Man's, must be the Soul,
And Reason the Inferior Powers control.
  Such were the Numbers which could call
  The Stones into the Theban wall.
Such Miracles are ceas'd; and now we see
Nor Towns or Houses rais'd by Poetry.

Yet 'tis not to adorn, and gild each part;
  That shows more Cost, than Art.
Jewels at Nose and Lips but ill appear;
Rather than all things Wit, let none be there.
  Several Lights will not be seen,
  If there be nothing else between.
Men doubt, because they stand so thick i' th'sky,
If those be Stars which paint the Galaxy.

'Tis not when two like words make up one noise;
  Jests for Dutch Men, and English Boys.
In which who finds out Wit, the same may see
In Anagrams and Acrostics Poetry.
  Much less can that have any place
  At which a Virgin hides her face,
Such Dross the Fire must purge away; 'tis just
The Author Blush, there where the Reader must.

'Tis not such Lines as almost crack the Stage
  When Bajazet begins to rage.
Nor a tall Metaphor in the Bombast way,
Nor the dry chips of short lung'd Seneca.
  Nor upon all things to obtrude,
  And force some odd Similitude.
What is it then, which like the Power Divine
We only can by Negatives define?

In a true piece of Wit all things must be,
    Yet all things there agree.
As in the Ark, join'd without force or strife,
All Creatures dwelt; all Creatures that had Life.
    Or as the Primitive Forms of all
    (If we compare great things with small)
Which without Discord or Confusion lie,
In that strange Mirror of the Deity.

Note. 'Bajazet': Turkish Emperor in Marlowe's *Tamburlaine the Great*.
He dies by breaking his skull on the bars of the cage in which he is
imprisoned.

Cowley finally defines wit (i.e. imagination) in a way which
does not differ fundamentally from Coleridge's in the *Biographia
Literaria* (ch. xiv): 'He [the poet] diffuses a tone and spirit of
unity, that blends, and (as it were) *fuses* each into each, by that
synthetic and magical power, to which I would exclusively
appropriate the name of Imagination. This power . . . reveals
itself in the balance or reconcilement of opposite or discordant
qualities: of sameness, with difference; of the general with the
concrete; . . . a more than usual state of emotion with more
than usual order.' Yet Cowley stands poised between the Meta-
physicals and the Augustans; and while there are elements in
this poem which remind us of the intellectual and emotional
excitement that we find in Donne, there are other elements
(particularly the balanced, antithetical syntax) which remind
us of the succeeding age, when reason would loom too large and
poetry too often be reduced to mere 'gilding'—'finny tribe'
instead of 'fish'. The ode uneasily (but interestingly) straddles
a chasm between two cultures.

from *Paradise Lost*, I, 1–26

Of Man's First Disobedience, and the Fruit
Of that Forbidd'n Tree, whose mortal taste
Brought Death into the World, and all our woe,
With loss of *Eden*, till one greater Man
Restore us, and regain the blissful Seat,
Sing Heav'nly Muse, that on the secret top
Of *Oreb*, or of *Sinai*, didst inspire
That Shepherd, who first taught the chosen Seed,
In the Beginning how the Heav'ns and Earth
Rose out of *Chaos*: or if *Sion* Hill
Delight thee more, and *Siloa*'s Brook that flow'd
Fast by the Oracle of God; I thence
Invoke thy aid to my advent'rous Song,
That with no middle flight intends to soar
Above th'*Aonian* Mount; while it pursues
Things unattempted yet in Prose or Rime.
And chiefly Thou O Spirit, that dost prefer
Before all Temples th'upright heart and pure,
Instruct me, for Thou know'st; Thou from the first
Wast present, and with mighty wings outspread
Dove-like satst brooding on the vast Abyss
And mad'st it pregnant: What in me is dark
Illumine, what is low raise and support;
That to the heighth of this great Argument
I may assert Eternal Providence,
And justify the ways of God to men.

What a deep breath, literally as well as metaphorically, Milton's
verse takes as he begins his epic. The long, involved opening
sentence, its main clause seeming always to be gliding ahead,
evading capture, *wills* the poem to take flight, unimpeded by the
slight checking tendency which rhyme would have had. Breath
and inspiration are one here, as they are semantically.

from *Rejoice in the Lamb*

For the spiritual musick is as follows.

For there is the thunder-stop, which is the voice of God
  direct.
For the rest of the stops are by their rhimes.
For the trumpet rhimes are sound bound, soar more and the
  like.
For the Shawn rhimes are lawn fawn moon boon and the like.
For the harp rhimes are sing ring, string & the like.

For the cymbal rhimes are bell well toll soul & the like.
For the flute rhimes are tooth youth suit mute & the like.
For the dulcimer rhimes are grace place beat heat & the like.
For the Clarinet rhimes are clean seen and the like.
For the Bassoon rhimes are pass, class and the like. God be
  gracious to Baumgarden.
For the dulcimer are rather van fan & the like and grace
  place &c are of the bassoon.
For beat heat, weep peep &c are of the pipe.
For every word has its marrow in the English tongue for
  order and for delight.

For the dissyllables such as able, table &c are the fiddle
  rhimes.
For all dissyllables and some trissyllables are fiddle rhimes.

Note. Baumgar(t)en was an eighteenth-century German philosopher
who established aesthetics as a study.

'Mad' Christopher Smart knew a hawk from a handsaw, yet he
was mad enough to correct the over-sane bias of the eighteenth
century and write some startling poetry, especially *Rejoice in the
Lamb* and *A Song of David*. Truly 'every word has its marrow',
but it may take a poet to sense it; for example, no poet before
or since has honoured the humble word 'for' with such exciting
(yet logically superfluous) use. He employs it with even greater
effect elsewhere in *Rejoice in the Lamb*, the famous passage begin-
ning 'For I will consider my cat Geoffrey'.

'Hear the voice of the Bard'

Hear the voice of the Bard,
Who Present, Past, & Future sees,
Whose ears have heard
The Holy Word
That walk'd among the ancient trees,

Calling the lapsed Soul,
And weeping in the evening dew—
That might controll
The starry pole
And fallen, fallen light renew!

'O Earth, O Earth, return!
Arise from out the dewy grass
Night is worn,
And the morn
Rises from the slumberous mass.

'Turn away no more.
Why wilt thou turn away?
The starry floor,
The wat'ry shore
Is giv'n thee till the break of day.'

I am reminded of those American Indian myths in which the
Word comes up out of the darkness even before the gods; of the
Navajo priest, Old Torlino, who guaranteed the solemn truth
of what he was to say by pointing out the inescapable watchful-
ness of the Word (which by its nature cannot lie): 'I am ashamed
before that standing within me which speaks with me. / Some
of these things are always looking at me. / I am never out of
sight. / Therefore I must tell the truth. / I hold my word tight
to my breast.' It is not only the subject of the poem which
relates it to that primitive, and seemingly outmoded, respect
for the purity of language; and not only that it takes the form
of a prayer or healing-spell, including the use of incantatory

'thought-rhymes' (e.g. 'Turn away no more: / Why wilt thou turn away?'): even more, it is the extraordinary sense that the words of the poem have all sprung immediately, dazzled by the light, into creation. One can partly explain this feeling, no doubt, by the high proportion of archetypes—earth, light, weep, grass, dew, soul, trees, night, stars, daybreak. If it were a painting, it would be wholly in primary colours. But having said that, I don't feel that the mystery has been penetrated very far.

Sonnet

Nuns fret not at their convent's narrow room;
And hermits are contented with their cells;
And students with their pensive citadels;
Maids at the wheel, the weaver at his loom,
Sit blithe and happy; bees that soar for bloom,
High as the highest Peak of Furness-fells,
Will murmur by the hour in foxglove bells:
In truth the prison, unto which we doom
Ourselves, no prison is: and hence for me,
In sundry moods, 'twas pastime to be bound
Within the Sonnet's scanty plot of ground;
Pleased if some Souls (for such there needs must be)
Who have felt the weight of too much liberty,
Should find brief solace there, as I have found.

———————

Wordsworth's sonnet on the sonnet seems to me to have a tired
and pallid feeling which makes it an ambiguous tribute. It
contains an implicit warning that the sonnet will at least have
to be moved away from its traditional forms (Shakespearean
and, as in this case, Petrarchan) if it is to serve the needs of poets
and readers in a 'dynamic', industrial and post-industrial
society. Nuns, in fact, *have* started to fret! Hopkins's sonnets,
with their freer rhythms, Yeats's magnificent *Leda and the Swan*
(traditional in form but with an untraditional violence in
theme), and recent experiments by John Berryman and Robert
Lowell, demonstrate the attempt at renewal.

'There was a Boy'

There was a Boy, ye knew him well, ye Cliffs
And Islands of Winander! many a time
At evening, when the stars had just begun
To move along the edges of the hills,
Rising or setting, would he stand alone
Beneath the trees, or by the glimmering Lake,
And there, with fingers interwoven, both hands
Press'd closely, palm to palm, and to his mouth
Uplifted, he, as through an instrument,
Blew mimic hootings to the silent owls
That they might answer him.—And they would shout
Across the watery Vale, and shout again,
Responsive to his call, with quivering peals,
And long halloos, and screams, and echoes loud
Redoubled and redoubled; concourse wild
Of mirth and jocund din! And when it chanced
That pauses of deep silence mock'd his skill,
Then sometimes, in that silence, while he hung
Listening, a gentle shock of mild surprise
Has carried far into his heart the voice
Of mountain torrents; or the visible scene
Would enter unawares into his mind
With all its solemn imagery, its rocks,
Its woods, and that uncertain Heaven, receiv'd
Into the bosom of the steady Lake.
  This boy was taken from his mates, and died
In childhood, ere he was full twelve years old.
Pre-eminent in beauty is the vale
Where he was born and bred: the churchyard hangs
Upon a slope above the village-school;
And through that churchyard when my way has led
On summer-evenings, I believe that there
A long half-hour together I have stood
Mute—looking at the grave in which he lies!

Wordsworth's poem explores the feminine aspect of creation, present in every child and every poet: the slow, quiet reception of images and experiences into one's breast, 'into the bosom of the steady lake', to be stored there in readiness. At the end, the simplicity of Wordsworth's genius allows no trace of irony or bitterness to lessen the effect of pure tragedy. Simply, this is how things are: 'the clay grows tall' merely, perhaps, to die. And in a poet, even one as great as Wordsworth, the 'hiding-places of his power' may unpredictably close.

Ode on a Grecian Urn

Thou still unravish'd bride of quietness,
　Thou foster-child of silence and slow time,
Sylvan historian, who canst thus express
　A flowery tale more sweetly than our rhyme!
What leaf-fringed legend haunts about thy shape
　Of deities or mortals, or of both,
　　In Tempe or the dales of Arcady?
　What men or gods are these? What maidens loath?
What mad pursuit? What struggle to escape?
　　What pipes and timbrels? What wild ecstasy?

Heard melodies are sweet, but those unheard
　Are sweeter; therefore, ye soft pipes, play on;
Not to the sensual ear, but, more endear'd,
　Pipe to the spirit ditties of no tone.
Fair youth, beneath the trees, thou canst not leave
　Thy song, nor ever can those trees be bare;
　　Bold Lover, never, never canst thou kiss,
　Though winning near the goal—yet, do not grieve;
She cannot fade, though thou hast not thy bliss,
　　For ever wilt thou love, and she be fair!

Ah, happy, happy boughs, that cannot shed
　Your leaves, nor ever bid the Spring adieu;
And, happy melodist, unwearied,
　For ever piping songs for ever new!
More happy love, more happy, happy love!
　For ever warm and still to be enjoy'd,
　　For ever panting and for ever young—
All breathing human passion far above,
That leaves a heart high-sorrowful and cloy'd,
　　A burning forehead, and a parching tongue.

Who are these coming to the sacrifice?
   To what green altar, O mysterious priest,
Lead'st thou that heifer lowing at the skies,
   And all her silken flanks with garlands drest?
What little town by river or sea shore,
   Or mountain-built with peaceful citadel,
      Is emptied of this folk, this pious morn?
   And, little town, thy streets for evermore
Will silent be; and not a soul to tell
      Why thou art desolate, can e'er return.

O Attic shape! Fair attitude! with brede
   Of marble men and maidens overwrought,
With forest branches and the trodden weed—
   Thou, silent form, dost tease us out of thought
As doth eternity: Cold Pastoral!
   When old age shall this generation waste,
      Thou shalt remain, in midst of other woe
   Than ours, a friend to man, to whom thou say'st,
'Beauty is truth, truth beauty'—that is all
      Ye know on earth, and all ye need to know.

———————

Ode on a Grecian Urn takes us below the world of change to
regions of art where the physically unreal is compensated for
by its permanence. The tensions of this state are the theme of
the poem, and seem close to the source of art's power to move
us. The still (adjective and adverb) unravished bride turns
constantly in the mind, like the urn itself, disturbing and
consoling simultaneously. The whole poem has a bridal
sensuality chastely restrained, its 'overwrought' feelings held in
check by the decorum suggested by the other meaning of over-
wrought—'embroidered on'. In the fourth stanza, we are drawn
down a vista of unparalleled distance, yet never does the scene
lose its clarity and focus: through the print, facing us yet apart
from us; to dead John Keats's mind as he wrote; to the urn he
pondered; to the maker of the urn; to the priest, worshippers

and sacrificial beast that he imagined and created; to the imagined town which the imagined people have left. In the last transformation, the town seems to come alive in its solitude, from the tender way in which Keats addresses it, and from the human associations of the word 'desolate'. We have been taken into an even more mysterious depth of experience than in R. M. Rilke's epitaph: 'ROSE, OH THE PURE CONTRADICTION, DELIGHT OF BEING NO-ONE'S SLEEP UNDER SO MANY LIDS'. And Keats's ode retains a human warmth; placing a supreme value on poetry, it does not make of it an ivory tower.

from *A Song of Mysel*

I

I celebrate myself, and sing myself,
And what I assume you shall assume,
For every atom belonging to me as good belongs to you.

I loafe and invite my soul,
I lean and loafe at my ease observing a spear of summer
    grass.

My tongue, every atom of my blood, form'd from this soil,
    this air,
Born here of parents born here from parents the same, and
    their parents the same,
I, now thirty-seven years old in perfect health begin,
Hoping to cease not till death.
Creeds and schools in abeyance,
Retiring back a while sufficed at what they are, but never
    forgotten,
I harbor for good or bad, I permit to speak at every hazard,
Nature without check with original energy.

2

Houses and rooms are full of perfumes, the shelves are
    crowded with perfumes,
I breathe the fragrance myself and know it and like it,
The distillation would intoxicate me also, but I shall not let it.

The atmosphere is not a perfume, it has no taste of the
    distillation, it is odorless,
It is for my mouth forever, I am in love with it,
I will go to the bank by the wood and become undisguised
    and naked,
I am mad for it to be in contact with me.

The smoke of my own breath,
Echoes, ripples, buzz'd whispers, love-root, silk-thread,
   crotch and vine,
My respiration and inspiration, the beating of my heart, the
   passing of blood and air through my lungs,
The sniff of green leaves and dry leaves, and of the shore
   and dark-color'd sea-rocks, and of hay in the barn,
The sound of the belch'd words of my voice loos'd to the
   eddies of the wind,
A few light kisses, a few embraces, a reaching around of arms,
The play of shine and shade on the trees as the supple
   boughs wag,
The delight alone or in the rush of the streets, or along the
   fields and hill-sides,
The feeling of health, the full-noon trill, the song of me rising
   from bed and meeting the sun.

Have you reckon'd a thousand acres much? have you
   reckon'd the earth much?
Have you practis'd so long to learn to read?
Have you felt so proud to get at the meaning of poems?

Stop this day and night with me and you shall possess the
   origin of all poems,
You shall possess the good of the earth and sun, (there are
   millions of suns left,)
You shall no longer take things at second or third hand, nor
   look through the eyes of the dead, nor feed on the
   spectres in books,
You shall not look through my eyes either, nor take things
   from me,
You shall listen to all sides and filter them from your self.

I am the poet of the Body and I am the poet of the Soul,
The pleasures of heaven are with me and the pains of hell
    are with me,
The first I graft and increase upon myself, the latter I
    translate into a new tongue.
I am the poet of the woman the same as the man,
And I say it is as great to be a woman as to be a man,
And I say there is nothing greater than the mother of men.

I chant the chant of dilation or pride,
We have had ducking and deprecating about enough,
I show that size is only development.

Have you outstript the rest? are you the President?
It is a trifle, they will more than arrive there every one, and
    still pass on.

I am he that walks with the tender and growing night,
I call to the earth and sea half-held by the night.

Press close bare-bosom'd night—press close magnetic
    nourishing night!
Night of south winds—night of the large few stars!
Still nodding night—mad naked summer night.

Smile O voluptuous cool-breath'd earth!
Earth of the slumbering and liquid trees!
Earth of departed sunset—earth of the mountains misty-topt!
Earth of the vitreous pour of the full moon just tinged with
    blue!
Earth of shine and dark mottling the tide of the river!
Earth of the limpid gray of clouds brighter and clearer for
    my sake!
Far-swooping elbow'd earth—rich apple-blossom'd earth!
Smile, for your lover comes.

Prodigal, you have given me love—therefore I to you give
    love!
O unspeakable passionate love.

Reading this poem, and perhaps comparing it with his American successor Wallace Stevens's very different 'rage for order' (**65**), we can see that free verse, which Whitman introduced, was his only logical form. Anything more regulated would not permit 'nature without check with original energy' to speak; for poetry to him had to be as generously all-embracing as America. And yet his free verse is not really 'free': we immediately recognize it as Whitman's and no one else's, which shows that it is not at all lawless. It may not obey the local by-laws, but it is within the constitution of poetry.

No form is ever really invented, just as nobody (whether Columbus or Leif the Lucky) 'first' landed in America. Christopher Smart in *Rejoice in the Lamb* (see **44**[**c**], **59**) wrote 'free verse' more than a century before Whitman, echoing the Psalms in the Authorized Version of the Bible.

The Idea of Order at Key West

She sang beyond the genius of the sea.
The water never formed to mind or voice,
Like a body wholly body, fluttering
Its empty sleeves; and yet its mimic motion
Made constant cry, caused constantly a cry,
That was not ours although we understood,
Inhuman, of the veritable ocean.

The sea was not a mask. No more was she.
The song and water were not medleyed sound
Even if what she sang was what she heard,
Since what she sang was uttered word by word.
It may be that in all her phrases stirred
The grinding water and the gasping wind;
But it was she and not the sea we heard.

For she was the maker of the song she sang.
The ever-hooded, tragic-gestured sea
Was merely a place by which she walked to sing.
Whose spirit is this? we said, because we knew
It was the spirit that we sought and knew
That we should ask this often as she sang.

If it was only the dark voice of the sea
That rose, or even colored by many waves;
If it was only the outer voice of sky
And cloud, of the sunken coral water-walled,
However clear, it would have been deep air,
The heaving speech of air, a summer sound
Repeated in a summer without end
And sound alone. But it was more than that,
More even than her voice, and ours, among
The meaningless plungings of water and the wind,
Theatrical distances, bronze shadows heaped
On high horizons, mountainous atmospheres
Of sky and sea.

It was her voice that made
The sky acutest at its vanishing.
She measured to the hour its solitude.
She was the single artificer of the world
In which she sang. And when she sang, the sea,
Whatever self it had, became the self
That was her song, for she was the maker. Then we,
As we beheld her striding there alone,
Knew that there never was a world for her
Except the one she sang and, singing, made.

Ramon Fernandez, tell me, if you know,
Why, when the singing ended and we turned
Toward the town, tell why the glassy lights,
The lights in the fishing boats at anchor there,
As the night descended, tilting in the air,
Mastered the night and portioned out the sea,
Fixing emblazoned zones and fiery poles,
Arranging, deepening, enchanting night.

Oh! Blessed rage for order, pale Ramon,
The maker's rage to order words of the sea,
Words of the fragrant portals, dimly-starred,
And of ourselves and of our origins,
In ghostlier demarcations, keener sounds.

Key West is on the coast of Florida.

Like *Ode on a Grecian Urn*, this poem is about the relationship
of imagination and external reality. The human imagination,
the woman singing by the shore, makes her song out of 'the
grinding water and the gasping wind', but articulates them,
orders them: and it is her song we listen to. The sea loses itself
in her song, until we know 'that there never was a world for her /
Except the one she sang and, singing, made'. Even the lights
of the fishing boats at anchor, reflecting on the sea, master the
night, mark out the darkness.

Such sovereignty for human order, supported by the sonorous
weight of Stevens's diction, might seem too enclosed and re-
stricting, quite frightening even; but the order is subtly balanced

by the potent mystery still of sea and woman—they survive ordering and definition and, in so doing, provide a necessary freedom. Another touch of freedom is offered by the unexplained intrusion of 'Ramon Fernandez', 'pale Ramon'. Admittedly, a literary scholar might be aware that Ramon Fernandez was a philosopher-critic; but in terms of the poem, and for the general reader, he breaks in anarchically, just as a hurricane might break and smash the fishing-boats. There is more tension, and therefore more life, in this poem than might at first appear. The imagination is not so dominant that a '*rage* for order' is not constantly needed.

Byzantium

The unpurged images of day recede;
The Emperor's drunken soldiery are abed;
Night resonance recedes, night-walkers' song
After great cathedral gong;
A starlit or a moonlit dome disdains
All that man is,
All mere complexities,
The fury and the mire of human veins.

Before me floats an image, man or shade,
Shade more than man, more image than a shade;
For Hades' bobbin bound in mummy-cloth
May unwind the winding path;
A mouth that has no moisture and no breath
Breathless mouths may summon;
I hail the superhuman;
I call it death-in-life and life-in-death.

Miracle, bird or golden handiwork,
More miracle than bird or handiwork,
Planted on the star-lit golden bough,
Can like the cocks of Hades crow,
Or, by the moon embittered, scorn aloud
In glory of changeless metal
Common bird or petal
And all complexities of mire or blood.

At midnight on the Emperor's pavement flit
Flames that no faggot feeds, nor steel has lit,
Nor storm disturbs, flames begotten of flame,
Where blood-begotten spirits come
And all complexities of fury leave,
Dying into a dance,
An agony of trance,
An agony of flame that cannot singe a sleeve.

Astraddle on the dolphin's mire and blood,
Spirit after spirit! The smithies break the flood,
The golden smithies of the Emperor!
Marbles of the dancing floor
Break bitter furies of complexity,
Those images that yet
Fresh images beget,
That dolphin-torn, that gong-tormented sea.

In 1929 Yeats had been seriously ill, and the following year he wrote *Byzantium* to 'warm himself back into life'. Midnight (as often in Yeats) is emblematic of the moment of dying; the 'gong' is both the tolling bell from great-domed Saint Sophia, and God's stroke from the dome of heaven. Time is being changed into eternity. The souls, traditionally, are being carried on the backs of dolphins—creatures of two elements—into paradise.

At another level, the chaos of experience is being hammered into art, into this poem, dying 'into a dance, / An agony of trance'; dance being a Yeatsian symbol for controlled passion. The process is not completed. In the end, the images are still tumbling in, on 'that dolphin-torn, that gong-tormented sea'—paradoxically, the last line is denser with life-energy than any other in the poem. It is a sign of a great poem that it resonates with meanings unspoken, pressing to enter it.

67 HUGH MACDIARMID

In the Fall, from *In Memoriam James Joyce*

Let the only consistency
In the course of my poetry
Be like that of the hawthorn tree
Which in early Spring breaks
Fresh emerald, then by nature's law
Darkens and deepens and takes
Tints of purple-maroon, rose-madder and straw.

Sometimes these hues are found
Together, in pleasing harmony bound.
Sometimes they succeed each other. But through
All the changes in which the hawthorn is dight,
No matter in what order, one thing is sure
—The haws shine ever the more ruddily bright!

And when the leaves have passed
Or only in a few tatters remain
The tree to the winter condemned
                    Stands forth at last
            Not bare and drab and pitiful,
But a candelabrum of oxidized silver gemmed
By innumerable points of ruby
Which dominate the whole and are visible
Even at considerable distance
As flame-points of living fire.
That so it may be
With my poems too at last glance
Is my only desire.
All else must be sacrificed to this great cause.
I fear no hardships. I have counted the cost.
I with my heart's blood as the hawthorn with its haws
Which are sweetened and polished by the frost!

See how these haws burn, there down the drive,
In this autumn air that feels like cotton wool,
When the earth has the gelatinous limpness of a body dead
        as a whole
While its tissues are still alive!

Poetry is human existence come to life,
The glorious energy that once employed
Turns all else in creation null and void,
The flower and fruit, the meaning and goal,
Which won all else is needs removed by the knife
Even as a man who rises high
Kicks away the ladder he has come up by.

This single-minded zeal, this fanatic devotion to art
Is alien to the English poetic temperament no doubt,
'This narrowing intensity' as the English say,
But I have it even as you had it, Yeats, my friend,
And would have it with me as with you at the end,
I who am infinitely more un-English than you
And turn Scotland to poetry like those women who
In their passion secrete and turn to
Musk through and through!

So I think of you, Joyce, and of Yeats and others who are
        dead
As I walk this Autumn and observe
The birch tremulously pendulous in jewels of cairngorm
The sauch, the osier, and the crack-willow
Of the beaten gold of Australia;
The sycamore in rich straw-gold;
The elm bowered in saffron;
The oak in flecks of salmon gold;
The beeches huge torches of living orange.

Billow upon billow of autumnal foliage
From the sheer high bank glass themselves
Upon the ebon and silver current that floods freely
Past the shingle shelves.
I linger where a crack willow slants across the stream,
Its olive leaves slashed with fine gold.
Beyond the willow a young beech
Blazes almost blood-red,
Vying in intensity with the glowing cloud of crimson
That hangs about the purple bole of a gean
Higher up the brae face.

And yonder, the lithe green-grey bole of an ash, with its
    boughs
Draped in the cinnamon-brown lace of samara.
(And I remember how in April upon its bare twigs
The flowers came in ruffs like the unshorn ridges
Upon a French poodle—like a dull mulberry at first,
Before the first feathery fronds
Of the long-stalked, finely-poised, seven-fingered leaves)—
Even the robin hushes his song
In these gold pavilions.
Other masters may conceivably write
Even yet in C major
But we—we take the perhaps 'primrose path'
To the dodecaphonic bonfire.

They are not endless these variations of form
Though it is perhaps impossible to see them all.
It is certainly impossible to conceive one that doesn't exist.
But I keep trying in our forest to do both of these,
And though it is a long time now since I saw a new one
I am by no means weary yet of my concentration
On phyllotaxis here in preference to all else,
All else—but my sense of sny!

The gold edging of a bough at sunset, its pantile way
Forming a double curve, tegula and imbrex in one,
Seems at times a movement on which I might be borne
Happily to infinity; but again I am glad
When it suddenly ceases and I find myself
Pursuing no longer a rhythm of duramen
But bouncing on the diploe in a clearing between earth and
    air
Or headlong in dewy dallops or a moon-spairged fernshaw
Or caught in a dark dumosity, or even
In open country again watching an aching spargosis of stars.

Note. 'samara': the fruit of the tree; 'phyllotaxis': the arrangement
of leaves upon an axis or stem; 'sny': a shipbuilding term for the 'run'
of the hull of a ship; 'tegula': a scale-like structure covering the base
of the fore-wing in insects; 'imbrex': the unit of a system of over-
lapping, or imbrication; 'duramen': the heartwood of a tree;

'diploe': that part of the leaf which comes between the two layers of the epidermis; 'dumosity': that which is full of brambles and briers; 'spargosis': the distention of the breasts caused by too much milk.

The varying line lengths, rhythm and vocabulary—notice, for example, the magical leap from the flatly polemical to the piercingly sensual in the verse-paragraph starting 'This single-minded zeal . . .'—enact in themselves the poem's primary image of 'nature's law' creating the inevitable and unique form, in a tree or a poem. Seasonal changes are likewise related to the way a poet's style develops as he grows older. Is the difficult technical vocabulary of the last part a touch of self-indulgence, or does it serve the poem?

from *How Hard It Is to Keep from Being King When It's
in You and in the Situation*

[*A king and his son, weary of power, leave their country to become slaves at the
court of King Darius. The ex-king, by knowing the quintessence of all things,
swiftly becomes indispensable:*]

... 'Feed him another feast of recognition.'

And so it went with triumph after triumph
Till on a day the King, being sick at heart
(The King was temperamental like his cook,
But nobody had noticed the connection),
Sent for the ex-King in a private matter.
'You say you know the inwardness of men,
As well as of your hundred other things.
Dare to speak out and tell me about myself.
What ails me? Tell me. Why am I unhappy?'

'You're not where you belong. You're not a King
Of royal blood. Your father was a cook.'

'You die for that.'
     'No, you go ask your mother.'

His mother didn't like the way he put it,
'But yes,' she said, 'someday I'll tell you, dear.
You have a right to know your pedigree.
You're well descended on your mother's side,
Which is unusual. So many Kings
Have married beggar maids from off the streets.
Your mother's folks—'
     He stayed to hear no more,
But hastened back to reassure his slave
That if he had him slain it wouldn't be
For having lied but having told the truth.
'At least you ought to die for wizardry.
But let me into it and I will spare you.
How did you know the secret of my birth?'

'If you had been a King of royal blood,
You'd have rewarded me for all I've done
By making me your minister-vizier,
Or giving me a nobleman's estate.
But all you thought of giving me was food . . .
I picked you out a horse called Safety Third,
By Safety Second out of Safety First,
Guaranteed to come safely off with you
From all the fights you had a mind to lose.
You could lose battles, you could lose whole wars,
You could lose Asia, Africa, and Europe,
No one could get you: you would come through smiling.
You lost your army at Mosul. What happened?
You came companionless, but you came home.
Is it not true? And what was my reward?
This time an all-night banquet, to be sure,
But still food, food. Your one idea was food.
None but a cook's son could be so food-minded.
I knew your father must have been a cook.
I'll bet you anything that's all as King
You think of for your people—feeding them.'

But the King said, 'Haven't I read somewhere
There is no act more kingly than to give?
'Yes, but give character and not just food.
A King must give his people character.'

'They can't have character unless they're fed.'

'You're hopeless,' said the slave.
                                        'I guess I am;
I am abject before you,' said Darius.
'You know so much, go on, instruct me further.
Tell me some rule for ruling people wisely,
In case I should decide to reign some more.
How shall I give a people character?'

'Make them as happy as is good for them.
But that's a hard one, for I have to add:
Not without consultation with their wishes;
Which is the crevice that lets Progress in.
If we could only stop the Progress somewhere,
At a good point for pliant permanence,
Where Madison attempted to arrest it.
But no, a woman has to be her age,
A nation has to take its natural course
Of Progress round and round in circles
From King to Mob to King to Mob to King
Until the eddy of it eddies out.'

'So much for Progress,' said Darius meekly.
'Another word that bothers me is Freedom.
You're good at maxims. Say me one on Freedom.
What has it got to do with character?
My satrap Tissaphernes has no end
Of trouble with it in his Grecian cities
Along the Aegean coast. That's all they talk of.'

'Behold my son in rags here with his lyre,'
The ex-King said. 'We're in this thing together.
He is the one who took the money for me
When I was sold—and small reproach to him.
He's a good boy. 'Twas at my instigation.
I looked on it as a Carnegie grant
For him to make a poet of himself on
If such a thing is possible with money.
Unluckily it wasn't money enough
To be a test. It didn't last him out.
And he may have to turn to something else
To earn a living. I don't interfere.
I want him to be anything he has to.
He has been begging through the Seven Cities
Where Homer begged. He'll tell you about Freedom.
He writes free verse, I'm told, and he is thought
To be the author of the Seven Freedoms:
Free Will, Trade, Verse, Thought, Love, Speech, Coinage.
(You ought to see the coins done in Cos.)
His name is Omar. I as a Rhodes scholar

Pronounce it Homer with a Cockney rough.
Freedom is slavery some poets tell us.
Enslave yourself to the right leader's truth,
Christ's or Karl Marx', and it will set you free.
Don't listen to their play of paradoxes.
The only certain freedom's in departure.
My son and I have tasted it and know.
We feel it in the moment we depart
As fly the atomic smithereens to nothing.
The problem for the King is just how strict
The lack of liberty, the squeeze of law
And discipline should be in school and state
To insure a jet departure of our going
Like a pip shot from 'twixt our pinching fingers.'

'All this facility disheartens me.
Pardon my interruption; I'm unhappy.
I guess I'll have the headsman execute me
And press your father into being King.'

'Don't let him fool you: he's a King already.
But though almost all-wise, he makes mistakes.
I'm not a free-verse singer. He was wrong there.
I claim to be no better than I am.
I write real verse in numbers, as they say.
I'm talking not free verse but blank verse now.
Regular verse springs from the strain of rhythm
Upon a meter, strict or loose iambic.
From that strain comes the expression *strains of music*.
The tune is not that meter, not that rhythm,
But a resultant that arises from them.
Tell them Iamb, Jehovah said, and meant it.
Free verse leaves out the meter and makes up
For the deficiency by church intoning.
Free verse, so called, is really cherished prose,
Prose made of, given an air by church intoning.
It has its beauty, only I don't write it.
And possibly my not writing it should stop me
From holding forth on Freedom like a Whitman—
A Sandburg. But permit me in conclusion:
Tell Tissaphernes not to mind the Greeks.

The freedom they seek is by politics,
Forever voting and haranguing for it.
The reason artists show so little interest
In public freedom is because the freedom
They've come to feel the need of is a kind
No one can give them—they can scarce attain—
The freedom of their own material:
So, never at a loss in simile,
They can command the exact affinity
Of anything they are confronted with.
This perfect moment of unbafflement,
When no man's name and no noun's adjective
But summons out of nowhere like a jinni.
We know not what we owe this moment to.
It may be wine, but much more likely love—
Possibly just well-being in the body,
Or respite from the thought of rivalry.
It's what my father must mean by departure,
Freedom to flash off into wild connections.
Once to have known it, nothing else will do.
Our days all pass awaiting its return.
You must have read the famous valentine
Pericles sent Aspasia in absentia:

> For God himself the height of feeling free
> Must have been His success in simile
> When at sight of you He thought of me.

Let's see, where are we? Oh, we're in transition,
Changing an old King for another old one.
What an exciting age it is we live in—
With all this talk about the hope of youth
And nothing made of youth. Consider me,
How totally ignored I seem to be.
No one is nominating me for King.
The headsman has Darius by the belt
To lead him off the Asiatic way
Into oblivion without a lawyer.
But that is as Darius seems to want it.

No fathoming the Asiatic mind.
And father's in for what we ran away from.
And superstition wins'. He blames the stars,
Aldebaran, Capella, Sirius
(As I remember they were summer stars
The night we ran away from Ctesiphon),
For looking on and not participating.
(Why are we so resentful of detachment?)
But don't tell me it wasn't his display
Of more than royal attributes betrayed him.
How hard it is to keep from being King
When it's in you and in the situation.
And that is half the trouble with the world
(Or more than half I'm half inclined to say).'

This poem was written in Frost's old age, yet it has an astonishing youthful energy. It is like a man turning double somersaults on a tightrope. Outrageous anachronistic puns, aphorisms about politics, freedom and poetry, in the guise of a folk-tale of a king and his son travelling as beggars: Frost seems capable of any dazzling brilliance. He *is* on a tightrope: if it were not for the strictness of the form he has chosen, blank verse, he would not be able to astonish us with such freedom. He once said that free verse was like playing tennis with the net down. He is not quite so dismissive here: 'It has its beauty, only I don't write it.' The interdependence of metre and rhythm that he discusses is superbly achieved. The poem verifies its own thesis, that law and discipline, both in politics and in poetry, ensure 'a jet departure of our going'.

The Thought-Fox

I imagine this midnight moment's forest:
Something else is alive
Beside the clock's loneliness
And this blank page where my fingers move.

Through the window I see no star:
Something more near
Though deeper within darkness
Is entering the loneliness:

Cold, delicately as the dark snow,
A fox's nose touches twig, leaf;
Two eyes serve a movement, that now
And again now, and now, and now

Sets neat prints into the snow
Between trees, and warily a lame
Shadow lags by stump and in hollow
Of a body that is bold to come

Across clearings, an eye,
A widening deepening greenness,
Brilliantly, concentratedly,
Coming about its own business

Till, with a sudden sharp hot stink of fox
It enters the dark hole of the head.
The window is starless still; the clock ticks,
The page is printed.

———————————

The stealthy approach of a real fox; the flesh-stirring apprehension of a poem—any poem or this poem—emerging from the dark forest of the poet's unconscious and that even darker forest of the universe surrounding him; possibly even the onset of death: many experiences are fused in *The Thought-Fox*. The page—the snow, the sheet of paper, the newborn child perhaps —starts blank. In a short while, it is 'printed', complete and finished. And still no star is visible, and the clock ticks on in its loneliness.

Ted Hughes writes: 'I was sitting up late one snowy night in dreary lodgings in London. I had written nothing for a year or so but that night I got the idea I might write something and I wrote in a few minutes the following poem [*The Thought-Fox*]: the first "animal" poem I ever wrote' (*Poetry in the Making*).

I
the song
I walk here

———————

'The song is short because we know so much.'

(Papago woman)

———————